INTER-SECTION 2018: CHRYSALIS

CURRENCY PRESS
SYDNEY

Australian Theatre
for Young People

CURRENCY PLAYS

First published in 2018
by Currency Press Pty Ltd,
PO Box 2287, Strawberry Hills, NSW, 2012, Australia
enquiries@currency.com.au
www.currency.com.au

Introduction © Fraser Corfield, *Director's Note* © Rachel Chant, *Under the Sensor Light* © Madison Behringer, *Lights on the Water* © Joseph Brown, *#NoFilter* © Pippa Ellams, *Six Weeks* © Harry Goodlet, *Jester* © Liz Hobart, *The Witch in the Window* © Alexander Lee-Rekers, *Bin Chicken* © Madelaine Nunn, *Victoria's Secret Angel Virgin / Bakerz Delight* © Julia Rorke, *Get Gone* © David Stewart, *Cul-de-sac* © Phoebe Sullivan, *The Blood on Bloody Blood Ladder* © Gretel Vella (all © 2018).

COPYING FOR EDUCATIONAL PURPOSES

The Australian *Copyright Act 1968* (Act) allows a maximum of one chapter or 10% of this book, whichever is the greater, to be copied by any educational institution for its educational purposes provided that that educational institution (or the body that administers it) has given a remuneration notice to Copyright Agency (CA) under the Act.

For details of the CA licence for educational institutions contact CA, 11/66 Goulburn St, Sydney, NSW, 2000; tel: within Australia 1800 066 844 toll free; outside Australia 61 2 9394 7600; fax: 61 2 9394 7601; email: info@copyright.com.au

COPYING FOR OTHER PURPOSES

Except as permitted under the Act, for example a fair dealing for the purposes of study, research, criticism or review, no part of this book may be reproduced, stored in a retrieval system, or transmitted in any form or by any means without prior written permission. All enquiries should be made to the publisher at the address above.

Any performance or public reading of any play within this collection is forbidden unless a licence has been received from the author or the author's agent. The purchase of this book in no way gives the purchaser the right to perform any of these plays in public, whether by means of a staged production or a reading. All applications for public performance should be addressed to the author/s c/- ATYP, Pier 4/5 Hickson Rd, Walsh Bay, NSW, 2000; tel: 61 2 9270 2400; email: hello@atyp.com.au.

Cataloguing-in-publication data for this title is available from the National Library of Australia website: www.nla.gov.au

Typeset by Emma Rose Smith for Currency Press.
Front cover shows Monica Kumar.
Cover photography by Luke Stambouliah.
Graphic design by Justin Stambouliah.

Currency Press acknowledges the Traditional Owners of the Country on which we live and work. We pay our respects to all Aboriginal and Torres Strait Islander Elders, past and present.

Contents

Introduction by Fraser Corfield	v
Director's Note by Rachel Chant	vi

INTERSECTION: CHRYSALIS

Under the Sensor Light Madison Behringer	1
Lights on the Water Joseph Brown	6
#NoFilter Pippa Ellams	12
Six Weeks Harry Goodlet	16
Jester Liz Hobart	22
The Witch in the Window Alexander Lee-Rekers	28
Bin Chicken Madelaine Nunn	33
Victoria's Secret Angel Virgin / Bakerz Delight Julia Rorke	39
Get Gone David Stewart	44
Cul-de-sac Phoebe Sullivan	56
The Blood on Bloody Blood Ladder Gretel Vella	62
Author and Mentor Biographies	71

Introduction
Fraser Corfield

Australian Theatre for Young People (ATYP), the national youth theatre company, is committed to commissioning and developing plays that young people can perform. Our long-term vision is to create a body of work broad enough and specific enough to connect with every young Australian. At ATYP our work is not driven by a need to be educational, though we always support our productions with learning resources. We are looking to generate stories that hold an audience's attention because they are detailed, well-drafted, unexpected and driven by an underlying truth.

We believe all the best theatre is written to be enjoyed, both in the telling and in the watching. At times confronting, surprising, hilarious or deeply uncomfortable, these are stories that reflect the experiences of growing up and growing older. For that reason much of our work comes with a language and content warning. Like in life, not all the characters are well behaved.

Intersection is a collection of short stories for the stage written by some of Australia's leading young playwrights. Each year a selection of writers aged between 18 and 26 attend the National Studio, a week-long playwriting retreat lead by some of the nation's leading playwrights and dramaturges. During the week the group map out a place, event, action or theme that can link a range of teenage characters. They then write seven-minute scenes for 17-year-old actors. ATYP selects ten of these for production. Those pieces become *Intersection* – the point of connection for very different teenage lives.

Intersection is an annual program, each year offering new characters, situations and scenes. Following in the footsteps of ATYP's hugely successful monologues program *The Voices Project*, *Intersection* will build over the years to offer young actors a range of short plays with characters and situations they can understand and relate to. Because that is the fundamental starting point for strong acting. When a character speaks in a rhythm that you know in your bones, dealing with issues that surround you every day, in a world not unlike the one that you live in, then you can portray that character with the depth and detail they deserve.

Feel free to pick and choose between the pieces you read in this publication and those in other years. You are welcome to curate your own production of short works. Their purpose is to instil an excitement and love of theatre and the storytelling process. If you would like to discuss *Intersection* or any of our other plays further, don't hesitate to contact us.

Fraser Corfield is the Artistic Director of ATYP.

Director's Note
Rachel Chant

Fuelled by hormones, the caterpillar stops eating. It hangs upside-down and spins itself a cocoon or chrysalis, kick-starting the process of digesting itself, dissolving into a caterpillar soup and eventually rearranging itself into a butterfly.

At least, that's how it goes in my layman's understanding of butterfly biology.

The eleven scripts in *Intersection* take a peek inside this cocoon, or in this case, at a number of complex, destructive, hopeful and transformative human soups. They peer in at that unique moment before we're due to emerge, bursting into the fully formed adults we're destined to be.

Unlike caterpillars, who (I think) aren't sentient enough to know they're about to transform, the characters in these plays seem to have a sense that something is coming or, in fact, that they may already be in the midst of their own soupy-transition. They're deciding what to do next, where to go, how to be and who to be. Some of them yearn to be different, to go somewhere new, to be something new. For others, the knowledge that things can't stay the same forever isn't as easy, the battle of aspiration versus expectation feeding a desire to stay soupy a little while longer. In any case, there is no denying that something is going to shift, and it's up to them to decide how they're going to own it.

When tasked with directing these pieces, I was initially concerned with how I was ever going to create a cohesive world from ten disparate short plays. And yet, when I sat in a circle of young playwrights on the final day of the National Studio in September 2017, I was amazed at how so many different voices from all around the country could be both so individual and yet so interconnected.

In *Intersection: Chrysalis*, we hear eleven young voices coming together, finding this point of commonality. This chrysalis feels unique to each of us, and I'm sure it is different for everyone. And yet there is something in these individual explorations that feels inescapably and undeniably similar. We all stew in the same questions of identity, sex, belonging and responsibility. It is a shared experience that unites us, no matter how painfully lonely it can often feel.

*Rachel Chant is a Sydney-based director
and dramaturg specialising in new writing.*

Acknowledgements

ATYP would like to acknowledge the support of the Graeme Wood Foundation, without whom *Intersection* would not be possible. Thank you to John and Julie and all at the Bundanon Trust, and the 2017 National Studio mentors: Michele Lee, Stephen Carleton and Mary Rachel Brown.

Thank you to all the writers from the 2017 National Studio, who created such a wonderful environment in which to meet and create new work: Genevieve Atkins, Madison Behringer, Joseph Brown, Michael Andrew Collins, Pippa Ellams, Stuart Fong, Harry Goodlet, Liz Hobart, Steffan Lazar, Alexander Lee-Rekers, Samantha Maclean, Imogen McCluskey, Madelaine Nunn, Rhiannon Petersen, Julia Rorke, David Stewart, Phoebe Sullivan, Jean Tong and Gretel Vella.

Intersection: Chrysalis was first produced by the Australian Theatre for Young People at SBW Stables Theatre, Nimrod Street, Kings Cross, Sydney, on 31 January 2018, with the following cast:

Under the Sensor Light
MAXIE	Anika Bhatia
WARREN	Benjamin Tarlinton

Lights on the Water
ISA	Jeremi Campese
TIM	Benjamin Tarlinton

#NoFilter
PERFORMER	Caitlin Burley

Six Weeks
DENNIS	Brenton Bell
ROD	Jeremi Campese

Jester
LEILA	Clare Taylor
SPARKY	Claire Crighton

The Witch in the Window
BEC	Clare Taylor
SARAH	Margaret Thanos

Bin Chicken
CLAIRE	Claire Crighton
LUKE	Brenton Bell

Victoria's Secret Angel Virgin / Bakerz Delight
JESS	Margaret Thanos

Get Gone
PERFORMER	Brenton Bell
PERFORMER	Anika Bhatia
PERFORMER	Caitlin Burley
PERFORMER	Jeremi Campese
PERFORMER	Claire Crighton
PERFORMER	Clare Taylor
PERFORMER	Margaret Thanos

Cul-de-sac
    PERFORMER   Anika Bhatia

The Blood on Bloody Blood Ladder
    GRACE   Anika Bhatia
    MAISY   Caitlin Burley

Director, Rachel Chant
Set and Costume Designer, Tyler Hawkins
Lighting Designer, Emma Lockhart-Wilson
Sound Designer and Composer, Brett Smith
Dramaturg, Jane FitzGerald
Assistant Director, Rebecca Blake
Stage Manager, Lillian Hannah U

We encourage anyone producing and casting these works to consider performers from diverse backgrounds.

A name without dialogue next to it indicates a silence in which a character choses not to speak or is unable to speak.

A slash (/) indicates a point of overlap. If at the start of a line, it means the next line is spoken simultaneously.

A dash (—) indicates a point of interruption.

Under the Sensor Light
Madison Behringer

MAXIE *is a 17-year-old female. She is an only child, living with her sick mum in one of the old mansions in town. She likes* The Sims *and hates coffee but drinks it every day because the other girls have started doing it.*

WARREN *is a 17-year-old male. He lives in the housing commission estate in the industrial area of town. He likes footy, fishing and plays a game of chess every night with his dad. Warren is deaf, and should be played by an actor who is fluent in Auslan.*

MAXIE *and* WARREN *walk into the space and stand side-by-side, facing the audience. They each occupy their own time and space, perhaps unaware of each other, and deliver their lines monologue-style, directly to the audience.* WARREN *signs his lines while they are simultaneously spoken by a voiceover.*

MAXIE: Well actually when I met Waz I didn't realise he was deaf.

WARREN: I think the first time I saw Maxie she was up on the roof of one of the house-boats down near the lake. She was up there carrying on with one of her mates, protesting about the fish dying in the water or something.

MAXIE: I was out near the lake with Suz, she's the one that always wears the hats. We had climbed on top of the half-sunk houseboats out there and were trying to raise awareness for the marine life in that area.

WARREN: She was holding this sign, it was blue cardboard with this really shit drawing of a fish on it.

MAXIE: Suz and I had been up there for ages, but then we realised the tide had come in and we were freaking out about how to swim across to the wharf. We had our phones with us and I had this huge Country Road duffel bag full of stuff and it was a huge swim to the shore.

WARREN: I think the tide had come in since they jumped up there cos her and her friend were jumping up and down and waving at me. It wasn't very far out to the boat they were on so I took my shirt off and jumped in.

MAXIE: Anyway, we were yelling and waving at Waz because he was the first person to come along that wasn't seedy and over sixty. He saw us waving to him and just ripped off his shirt, ran along the wharf and started swimming out to us. He grabbed all our stuff, held it above his head and started swimming back. He was in front of us the whole time, and I kept rambling on about how he'd saved us, how he was so nice, thank you so much, we could have died, bla bla bla. And I thought he was just some arrogant prick with a six-pack because he completely ignored me.

WARREN: I can tell these two girls, Maxie and her mate Suz, I can tell that they're trying to talk to me. We're swimming along and I'm in front and each time I look back I can see Maxie's eyes shooting into me and her mouth's moving really quickly, half under water, half above, and I'm trying to read her bloody lips but she's talking too fast. I didn't know how to tell this girl that I couldn't read what she was saying. This crazy brown-haired mess of a chick who's trying to upload our swim across the lake to her Snapchat Story.

MAXIE: Once we got to the wharf I was ready to kind of brush him off, thank him again and then leg it. I mean he'd ignored us the whole time, I thought he was just being a dickhead because he could probably tell how hot I thought he was and wasn't into it. But then he turned around to us and just said, 'I wasn't ignoring you, I'm deaf.' I felt like such a knob. He was super nice about it though. Then I randomly bumped into him again at a house party at Holly's a few weeks later.

WARREN: She added me on Facebook the next day and invited me to a house-party on her street.

MAXIE: Suz was already eighteen at this point so she bought us a case of Cruisers to share. By the time Waz got there I was twerking to Rihanna and was drunk enough to pull him onto the lounge-room dance floor and shove a half-drunk bottle in his hand.

WARREN: I didn't know any of the kids at the party, they all go to the wanky private school, so I got my brother to get me a couple of longnecks from the BWS and kind of hung out the front by myself for a bit.

MAXIE: We'd gone out into the backyard so Waz could have a smoke… it was just the two of us out there. Me, Waz and his packet of cheap cigarettes.
WARREN: I went out the back at one point for a durry and Maxie kind of followed me out there. She was smashed hey, giggling and holding on to my arm when she talked to me. It was cute, her trying to talk to me. She'd slow down her sentences heaps cos I think she could tell I was trying to read her lips. She kept throwing her arms around like it was a game of charades, trying to help me understand. Normally that shit annoys me, but when she did it it was heaps different.
MAXIE: I'd kissed one guy before Warren and it was horrible. Remember that dare with Ryan? There was a bunch of tongue involved and he was wasted and nervous and it was gross. Then I'm standing in Holly Carter's backyard under the sensor light and I'm coughing my lungs up because I'm smoking my first cigarette so Waz thinks I'm cool and I'm begging him to kiss me. I'm actually saying out loud, 'I want you to kiss me' but he can't tell because he's looking at his phone and I mean he's deaf, so… [*Awkwardly*] yeah.
WARREN: So I'm standing there, and she's looking all cute and drunk and she's coughing her bloody guts up. I'd offered her a cig to be polite thinking for sure she'd say no, but she took it and looked like a newborn giraffe trying to walk for the first time as she's trying to light it, fumbling with the lighter and laughing heaps. Maxie was actually saying 'I want you to kiss me', thinking I couldn't see her lips mouthing the words, it was bloody hilarious. I pretended I was looking at my phone then waited for her to finish her cigarette before I kind of leant in, grabbed her chin and smacked one on her.
MAXIE: Have you ever kissed someone and just been like 'Holy shit I can't feel my legs'? That's what kissing Waz is like. I think that's the moment I started falling in love with him, right there out the back of Holly Carter's place with the sensor light switching off every now and again. After we made out for a bit we went back inside. A bunch of the guys were trying to get a group together to walk to the Ladder. Waz was holding my hand. He finds it hard to lip-read when people are drunk, because they slur their words and carry on like idiots. I felt warm, like I was the only one who could possibly help him communicate with the crowd of swarming

assholes. Dating Waz is nice, like that. You feel needed in a way that's so much more important and bigger than normal.

WARREN: We ended up at the Ladder with a bunch of Maxie's mates from the party. It leads up to the top of the big silo up there. The other lads we were with were playing footy with a can of VB and I was trying to convince Maxie to climb to the top of the silo with me cos you can sit up there and look out over the whole town.

MAXIE: Waz was halfway up the Ladder, climbing to the top of the silo when the guys start yelling out HEADS! HEADS! HEADS UP BRO and then I see the VB can flying toward him. I guess I kind of just forgot he couldn't hear them, because I was wondering why he wasn't ducking.

WARREN: Out of no-where this can of VB smacks me on the back of the head as I'm climbing up the ladder. Then all the dudes are running at me and pulling me off the ladder to check I'm okay, and they're behind me so I can't read what they're saying and one guy's trying to get me to shotgun the can of beer and none of them are realising I can't hear them and Maxie's trying to explain.

MAXIE: He ended up getting clobbered on the back of the head with the can of VB, I felt so bad. He was totally fine, but the boys hadn't realised he was deaf and were trying to rumble with him and it was all pretty hilarious. Mind you I was seven Cruisers down at this point.

WARREN: I had a bit of a rumble with the boys after and then Max and I watched the sun come up on top of the silo.

MAXIE: Yeah so that was… six months ago now? About that. It was really hard at first, with Waz being deaf. But then I learnt how to sign a bit and it's gotten better. I dunno though, it's almost like we speak different languages sometimes so it's tricky to have long conversations. A couple of times I've called him and totally forgotten he can't talk on the phone, so embarrassing. I just hope we last after we graduate this year. He wants to move to Sydney but you know, I'll have to stick around here to look after Mum.

WARREN: I do wanna move to Sydney after I graduate but her mum's pretty crook so she might have to stick around here for a bit. I know we'll work it out though, you don't find a chick like Maxie and then bugger off cos her mum's not well. We have our whole lives to move to different places, I'd rather wait and move with her than go myself and miss her every day.

MAXIE: I've never felt like this before though, so it has to work out, right? You don't find someone as lovely as him with a killer six-pack and then give up on it because you wanna live different places. I can't even imagine not seeing him every day now. I tell him all the time:

> *She signs to* WARREN, *also speaking the words: 'You're the best thing since sliced bread'.*

He's the best thing since sliced bread… I know it's lame, but he is.

Lights on the Water
Joseph Brown

TIM *and* ISA, *both 17.*

They stand at the edge of the lookout. The town lights are laid out before them. ISA *shivers slightly, and then checks his phone.* TIM *just looks out in wonder.*

ISA *shivers again.*

TIM: What's the matter?
ISA: It's fucking freezing.
TIM: It's November.
ISA: Then this place should start acting like it.
TIM: I think it's nice.

> ISA *shakes his head. He draws his jacket a little closer. He pulls out his phone, checks it. Nothing. He puts it back in his pocket.*

    So, what do you reckon?
ISA: About what?
TIM: This!
ISA: It's a lookout. I've seen a lookout before.

> *Pause.*

TIM: Yeah. Right.
ISA: Wait, was this what you brought me here for? Oh my god.
TIM: What?
ISA: This is it, isn't it? This is the main place to hang out?
TIM: I mean… No. There's others.
ISA: Oh yeah? Like what, the speedway?
TIM: … Yeah.
ISA: Fuck.
TIM: You don't like it?
ISA: There's nothing to like. It's a lookout.
TIM: I just thought you might want to get a good view of your new home.
ISA: This isn't my home.

TIM: Oh.

> *Pause.*

> You came from Sydney, yeah?

ISA: Against my will.

TIM: What did you do there?

ISA: More than I think you guys do here.

TIM: Oh. Cool.

> *Pause. The boys stand around awkwardly for a while. Not looking at each other.*

ISA: Have you ever been? To Sydney I mean?

TIM: Oh. Umm. Yeah. Just once.

ISA: Yeah? What did you think?

TIM: I can't really remember it. Too young I guess.

ISA: Yeah. Right.

> *Silence.*

TIM: Are you settling in okay at school? Not to sound like your parents or anything. I just mean. Umm.

ISA: Yeah. Yeah it's fine. Everyone seems nice enough.

TIM: Cool. I didn't know if you'd made any friends yet. So I thought I'd just, I dunno, extend the hand of friendship. Or something.

> ISA *just looks at* TIM.

> I'm rambling a bit. Sorry. I do that when I'm nervous.

ISA: Why are you nervous?

TIM: No reason.

> *Silence.*

> Hey, did you know that this place has witches? Like, spell-casting, child-eating witches.

ISA: Seriously?

TIM: On my life. See those old estates down there? Just behind all the new developments off the highway? Haunted.

ISA: Bullshit.

TIM: Could be. But it scared the hell out of us when we were kids.

ISA: And now?

TIM: I still take the long way home to avoid them when I can. But when

I was a kid I never walked past them in case they came out and punished me.

ISA: For what?

    Pause.

TIM: Did you know your way around in Sydney?

ISA: I mean, I knew how to get to where I needed to go.

TIM: What about all the back ways? The shortcuts? Stuff like that.

ISA: I dunno, maybe.

TIM: I know this place so well. I reckon I could draw a map of it no trouble. All the side streets and little hideaways.

ISA: Really?

TIM: Definitely. I'm always out wandering around. Ever since I was a kid. Didn't like being at home so I'd walk around. Eventually everything just became familiar to me. Every corner. Every pebble. It was all mine. That's how I knew when you moved in. Before I saw you in school, I mean. Something different was happening on the street. No moving truck, which I thought was weird.

ISA: We didn't have much stuff.

TIM: Right. That house you're in has been empty for ages.

ISA: I hate it.

TIM: You'll get used to it.

ISA: I'm only here for a year. That's it. One year then I'll be finished with school and straight back to Sydney. Back to real life.

TIM: This is real life.

ISA: No, this is a detour.

    ISA *checks his phone. Nothing.*

TIM: You know there's no reception up here, right?

    ISA *suddenly runs to the edge and screams out over the town:*

ISA: FUCK YOU ALL!!

TIM: Isa! Jesus, calm down!

ISA: They promised they wouldn't forget me. All my friends. They said they'd message me every day. So far it's been two weeks and there's been nothing. How can you just forget about someone so quickly?

    Silence.

TIM: I do remember going to Sydney. Once. I was little. Eleven or something. My brother was in the hospital and we were there for some treatment he was having. I can hardly remember it now. I think Mum and Dad were talking to the doctors, or something. I was bored, so I wandered off. Found my way to the exit. Walked outside. Wasn't thinking I guess. Just saw the door and left. I was outside, and I looked up and everything is just so tall. I can't believe it. I didn't know that you could build things that reached that high up into the sky. I'm kind of in awe of it, wandering around with my head craned up, trying to see the top. I lose where I am. And people start bumping into me. Even though I'm just a kid. Everyone just pushes past me. Suddenly I'm scared. I panic. I start crying. Huge sobs. I'm struggling to breathe through the sobbing.

ISA: What happened?

TIM: Just stood there and cried. My dad eventually found me. He was so angry at me.

ISA: Nobody stopped for you?

TIM: Nope.

ISA: Fuck.

TIM: Yeah. We just went back to the hospital and I wasn't allowed out of my parent's sight for the rest of the time. I just never wanted to feel lost again.

    Pause.

ISA: Your brother…

TIM: He was… umm, he was really sick. Really bad asthma. I don't know all the details. We never talk about it anymore. But yeah, he was there to see a specialist because he wasn't breathing properly.

    Pause.

ISA: Did he die?

TIM: Yeah. At the hospital.

ISA: I'm sorry.

TIM: It's okay. I don't really think about it much anymore.

ISA: Right.

TIM: Why did you agree to come up here with me?

ISA: I just couldn't spend another night in there. In that house. Dad is…

    Pause.

It's the same every night, you know? He'll just sit there and microwave the same stale cup of coffee over and over again. He'll watch the same infomercials all night long. And he'll tell me, 'This is it, Isa. This time I'm serious. I'm gonna buy a Thermomix'.

TIM: Where's your mum?

ISA: She's still in Sydney.

TIM: Oh.

ISA: Yeah. I'd say the divorce was getting to him, but to be honest, I think he's always been like this. It felt easy in Sydney. He was the same there as he is here. But back there, in the city, when I came home and heard him crying I could just turn around and leave. And there'd always be somewhere to go and something to do. But here… Here I have nightmares every night and wake up in a room I don't recognise. It's so… different. When you knocked on the door, I could already hear him in the kitchen, with the microwave going. And then you were standing there. I thought you were going to take me somewhere else. I thought you were going to help me escape. But mostly, I just thought you looked cute, standing in my doorway like that.

Pause.

I've seen you at school, you know? Looking at me.

TIM: I don't know what you're talking about.

Pause.

ISA: Are you going to kiss me?

Pause.

Is that what you do with all the boys? Bring them up here? Show them the speedway?

TIM: I… No. There haven't been any others.

ISA: Have you ever told anyone?

TIM: My brother. Just before he died. And when he was gone, my parents seemed to lose something in them. I didn't want to make anything harder for them.

ISA: It's fine, you know? That you feel this way. You know that, right?

TIM: I guess.

ISA: Are you worried what people will think?

TIM: I want to say no. That it doesn't affect me. That I'm stronger than that. But the truth is… Yeah. I'm terrified.

ISA: You thought they'd punish you. The witches.
TIM: Yeah.
> *Pause.*

ISA: Are you nervous?
TIM: Very.
ISA: It's okay.
TIM: I know.
> ISA *leans in and kisses* TIM. *The two pull each other close.*
> *They break apart slowly.*

Thanks.
ISA: You don't have to thank me. Dork.
TIM: I know. I wanted to.
ISA: Okay.
> *Pause. The two boys look out over the lights of the town.*

I'm not staying here. You know that, right?
TIM: Look out over there.
> TIM *points out towards the water.*

Look how the lights from Wet'n'Wild bounce off the water. Just over there.
ISA: What about it?
TIM: Just shut up and look at it.
> *They look at the lights dance on the water.*
> ISA *goes to reach for his phone.* TIM *stops him by taking hold of his hand. They hold hands and look out over the water.*

ISA: It's nice. Kind of.

#NoFilter
Pippa Ellams

Shower. Exfoliate. Shave. Shampoo. Conditioner. Moisturiser. Deodorant. Hair serum. Heat protecting spray. Blow dry. Tie it back. Cotton pad. Oil cleanse. Foam cleanse. Cotton pad. Tea tree oil, spots. Bio oil, scars. Cotton pad. Toner. Tap it in. Essence. Rub it in. Serum. Eye cream, use ring finger. Sunscreen. Moisturiser. Essence mist. Primer. Contour stick. Blend. Concealer. Blend. Foundation. Blend. Eyeshadow. Brows. Lashes. Eyeliner. Highlight. Powder. Setting spray. Straightener. Hair oil. Hairspray. Outfit Calvin Klein. Ripped jeans. Push up bra. Midriff white top. Hide the straps. Nikes. Nails. Necklace. Earrings. Rings. Handbag. Brush teeth. Lip kit. Done.

This is my Casual Look.

The aim is to look natural, seem apathetic, but still look hot.

These two sections here are my skin sections.

She points to her waist and boobs.

You can't have more than two skin sections or you just look trashy. If I showed leg, midriff and boob, it would be too much.

Emma in my class told me I was just a Kylie Jenner wannabe, as if it was a bad thing. Kylie Jenner has a net worth of fifty million. She is an entrepreneur. Emma's favourite artist works at Woolworths to pay rent.

Because of the way I look, a lot of the girls in class try to put me down. Saying I'm stupid or whatever. This girl Rebecca complains about putting on weight every day and orders sausage rolls and chips at lunchtime. Rebecca knows they make her fat and continues to eat them anyway. That's real stupidity.

Sometimes I want to help these people in my school. I want to tell

Emma if you tea-tree-oil your pimples instead of picking at them you won't look like a meth head with delicate eyebrow structure.

But that would be impolite.

I've learnt the key to having confidence in any situation is to always have an insult about someone's face ready. If they attack the outfit you've chosen just hit them with 'Oh Sadie, your face isn't as symmetrical as I thought it was'. I can change my outfit but they can't change their face.

I never used to bitch about anyone behind their back. I used to be able to see the good in everyone. That was until someone filmed me getting fingered behind the Tropical Cyclone at Wet'n'Wild.

Yeah so that happened.

But it's fucking fine.

If you fully accept that you're not a great person, then what?

'Bianca, you're a bitch.'

'Yes… I know.'

That's it. Shut down.

As long as you're aware of it, nothing can humiliate you.

'Your nose hairs are long for a girl.'

I know.

I know.

I know I know I know. I know every single thing wrong about me. I've made it a point to know. 'You have scars on the back of your legs.' I know. 'You have low-set ears on your face.' I know.

Go on. Try me.

I keep having the thought, if I look good enough he has to love me back?

I mean just, Elliot was my friend so clearly he liked my personality. So it must have been my face. And my body.

I'm going to be someone Elliot would be proud to finger. Looking back, I understand now why people said what they did. Why they commented what they commented... because it was true.

After everyone saw the Wet'n'Wild fingering video they didn't tease me. They teased him.

They teased Elliot for fingering such a pimply ugly whale of a girl.

That he must have looked into the sun that day or was aiming for quantity by lowering the quality.

Elliot didn't look at me for months after. He got his lip pierced and I didn't know because the last time I saw his face it looked like an embarrassed red melted candle as he tried to run after the boys with the iPhone.

But you know, like, it's understandable, I watched the footage. I wouldn't want to finger me either. That girl on the screen is clearly a stupid, silly little girl who just doesn't know how to do anything, her hair, her skin, go to the gym, fill her brows... She was just a fifteen-year-old with a Spongebob one-piece before Selena Gomez brought back one-pieces.

After Wet'n'Wild I couldn't walk into a classroom without feeling it.

The eyes. Looking at my double chin, my pimples, my Big W school bag. Zooming in. Judging me.

I knew, knew I would feel these eyes on me for the rest of my life.

From my boyfriend, my friends, people at work, going out and walking down the street from people I don't and will never know.

So if these eyes are gonna be on me, I need to feel good about them being on me.

Now when the eyes look at me usually they comment:

'What products do you use?'

'Where did you get this done?'

'You're so lucky to have that body, so lucky to have those lashes, so lucky to have hairless arms.' Lucky.

And if the comments aren't there I search for them.

I'm getting some fillers next month once I save enough. I'm very excited for the fillers. As you've probably noticed my lips are a little on the thin side.

I can't wait till Elliot sees them… but you know what, fuck Elliot. He looks like a stretched-out Danny DeVito with a vitamin D deficiency.

Beat.

God I'm fucking poison. I used to really like Elliot. I used to really like everyone. Just listening to me speak I hate it. How have you listened to me for so long?

I can't ever go back to Wet'n'Wild. I keep having this fear that if I actually ride down the Tropical Cyclone, something will happen and I'll go back to being that ugly, flubbery fifteen-year-old and I can never let that happen.

I don't like these products, doing a full contour every morning but I know I will feel worse if I don't.

And don't you dare try and say that I don't need it, that I'm beautiful without it. Because you don't say that. You say:

'You look tired today.'

'You feeling okay, you sick?'

And then when I do, you say 'You look great!'

So what should I do?

Elliot said Keira Knightley looked beautiful in that emerald-green dress in *Atonement* so now I have a whole wardrobe of emerald green. Such a hard colour to match with.

Elliot's eyes. His face. Those freshly-pierced lips. I hate that I care about his eyes the most and what they see. I want to tear them out. What about my eyes? What I see? When I look… shouldn't I? I?

God I'm so dramatic sometimes. I'm really fine. Yeah I fucking hate my life and so what. I know.

I know. I know so…

Six Weeks

Harry Goodlet

DENNIS *and* ROD *run onstage, each with a wheelbarrow covered with a tarp. They set them down and take a moment to catch their breath. Still on their haunches.* DENNIS *eventually lets out a laugh.*

DENNIS: I thought wheelbarrows were meant to make shit lighter.
ROD: Mine's fine. You took too many.
DENNIS: Let me see.

> DENNIS *lifts up* ROD'*s wheelbarrow.*

What the hell? Did you even get any?
ROD: I got heaps. C'mon, let's keep moving.
DENNIS: How do people run around with this shit all day? No wonder Jamie Durie got so ripped on that gardening show.
ROD: Pretty sure he was a stripper before he went on that show.
DENNIS: Really?
ROD: Yeah, that's why he's so hot.
DENNIS: He's hot because he was a stripper?
ROD: No, he was a stripper because he's hot.
DENNIS: But was he already ripped when he went into stripping or did the stripping get him ripped?
ROD: I dunno… I'll become a gardener, you become a stripper and we'll see who gets a better body.
DENNIS: We're already the best gardeners in this town.
ROD: I don't think this counts as gardening.

> ROD *kicks over the wheelbarrow, letting dozens of doormats spill onto the dirt.*

How long do you think it'll take people to realise?
DENNIS: [*in a posh accent*] All the uptowners will be getting on their bus to go to Clarendon College in approximately ninety minutes.
ROD: [*doing the same accent*] I'm sure they'll alert Mummy and Daddy immediately.

They both laugh.

How did you even come up with this?

DENNIS: Well. You know how Mullins gave me that detention the other day out of nowhere—

ROD: You stole fertiliser out of the maintenance shed to make a 'small bomb'.

DENNIS: Bullshit. It was for gardening. I told you, I'm a gardener.

ROD: Bullshit. Mullins found you smooshing three lit matches into a handful of soil behind the gym.

DENNIS: That was not wh—

ROD: How the fuck did you think that was going to work?

DENNIS: It's called trial and error, Rod, you dickhead.

ROD: Whatever. The doormats?

DENNIS: Right. So they made me go to this 'voluntary' economics revision seminar on Saturday, and I learnt something very interesting. First thing is that there are genuine freaks at our school who go to school on Saturday to learn more about economics.

ROD: That's gross.

DENNIS: However, this particular seminar did somewhat capture my attention, with a little phrase known as *insider trading*.

ROD: Go on.

DENNIS: Turns out, if you figure out that some shit is about to go down before it goes down, then all you have to do is put your money in the right places. Therefore—

ROD: We steal everybody's doormats, they have to go and buy new ones and we invest in whoever is selling them wholesale to Bunnings.

DENNIS: Almost. We go to Bunnings, buy all the doormats they have left and we give them to Stavros… Lawrence's little brother? He sets up a lemonade stall type thing, except for doormats, and sells them at sky-high prices. All he asks for is a ten percent cut, and the rest is ours.

ROD begins stacking the doormats.

ROD: Why don't we just cut him out and sell them ourselves?

DENNIS: Rod, we are literally the first two people that everyone will suspect stole their doormats. Remember when we were nine and Greenpeace freed all those dolphins from the aquarium and everyone thought it was us?

ROD: That was a tough week. Can we trust Stavros not to rat on us?

DENNIS: Stavros has been around the block. He knows when he's in on a good deal.

ROD: He's seven.

DENNIS: The kid's been selling counterfeit juice since he was four. Got suspended from pre-primary last year.

ROD: He's setting himself up for quite the reputation.

DENNIS: Rep is everything in this hole.

Beat.

ROD: What's your rep?

DENNIS: Can't really ask someone about their own reputation.

ROD: What's mine then?

DENNIS: We're too close for me to tell. You're the uglier half of Dennis and Rod.

ROD: So you have your own identity, but I'm just tacked onto you?

DENNIS: Eh, there are worse reps to have. You know how Joe Kerrigan's mum looks heaps like that science teacher Mrs Shiels? He got caught with a stiffy in her class one time and then everybody started calling him Oedipus.

ROD: You started calling him Oedipus.

DENNIS: I have my moments.

ROD: There's the little reader that peeks through every now and then.

DENNIS: What do you mean?

ROD: Anybody who's ever sat in an English class with you would be shocked to learn you've read the alphabet, let alone some old book that's not on the syllabus.

DENNIS: So what?

ROD: So why do you hide stuff like that?

DENNIS: I don't hide it. I tell you all the time.

ROD: But that's me.

DENNIS: Should I gather our class together and inform them of how well-read I am? We're not at Clarendon.

ROD: Oooh, I bet they read *Oedipus* at Clarendon. I think you would've looked great in that boy scout's uniform.

DENNIS: [*Laughing*] Piss off.

Beat.

Maybe I'll transfer for the last six weeks of the year.

ROD: Graduate from there and then you can get an internship at Goldworth's with one of Daddy's friends.

DENNIS: Gotta make sure that I come back to let all the locals know I'm better than they are. You've got to give back somehow.

ROD: Nothing says 'giving back to the community' like stealing their doormats.

DENNIS: We give back in the form of entertainment. Imagine how boring this place would be without us.

ROD: We'll find out next year I guess.

Silence.

DENNIS: I reckon I might hang around here for a bit longer.

ROD: Really?

DENNIS: Yeah.

ROD: I didn't know that.

DENNIS: It's never come up.

ROD: How long have you thought this?

DENNIS: A while.

ROD: Why didn't you say anything when we met with the careers guy?

DENNIS: Because I knew he'd tell me to apply myself and go for scholarships and shit.

ROD: Why don't you? We could both go to Sydney.

DENNIS: I dunno. Maybe.

DENNIS *begins fidgeting with the mats on the ground.*

ROD *lingers in slightly shocked silence.*

I don't know. I don't know what I want to do yet.

ROD: Okay.

DENNIS: What?

ROD: What what?

DENNIS: I knew this was going to happen.

ROD: What do you mean?

DENNIS: If I told you that I wasn't going to go, you would judge me.

ROD: I'm not judging you.

DENNIS: Are you applying?

ROD: Yeah, but I just want to keep my options open.

DENNIS: So do I.

ROD: That's good.

> *Silence.*

So what do you think you'll do next year? You should nick post boxes.

DENNIS: Fuck off.

ROD: It's a joke. What's wrong with you?

DENNIS: Just because I don't want to lie on the grass with my feet up, listen to Radiohead, and read Camus in between lectures means there's something wrong with me?

ROD: That's oddly specific. And that's not what I meant.

DENNIS: What did you mean?

ROD: Why are you so on edge?

DENNIS: Because I'm sick of people asking me what I'm doing next year and I know that everyone else is leaving.

ROD: It'll be different without everyone here.

DENNIS: Yeah.

ROD: Why don't you come up and try it and if you don't like it then you can just come—

DENNIS: Back home and have everybody looking at me like I'm some retard who couldn't hack it?

ROD: Right.

DENNIS: I kind of like being here.

ROD: I know. I'm just surprised. That's all.

DENNIS: Even though this place is kind of shit, its still kind of not shit.

ROD: You should put that in a scholarship essay.

> DENNIS *lobs a doormat at* ROD. *Beat.*

DENNIS: Are you definitely going?

ROD: I think so.

> *Silence.*

DENNIS: Would be pretty cool if you stayed.

ROD: Yeah…

> *Pause.*

One more year of the Dennis and Rod show.

> *Silence.*

DENNIS: Why do you want to go?
ROD: You remember Joe Vidler's funeral?
DENNIS: All I remember was that they called him the Fiddler the whole time and it made me uncomfortable.
ROD: That's why I want to go.
DENNIS: It's just a nickname.
ROD: That was all he was to everybody at that funeral. Everybody just knew him as that. There comes a point where someone will say your name for the last time, and then it'll never be said again. When was the last time you heard anyone talk about him? It's been six years and he's basically forgotten.

Pause.

DENNIS: I think the Fiddler will always be inside of us.

ROD *throws the doormat back at* DENNIS. *Beat.*

ROD: I don't think it'll be that scary. You'd probably be fine.
DENNIS: Probably.

Pause.

ROD *looks around.*

ROD: You're right, though. This place is shit… in a kind of non-shit way.
DENNIS: I don't really think it's this place.
ROD: Yeah. We could probably make living in a septic tank fun.
DENNIS: No doormats in there.
ROD: You know where else there are no doormats.
DENNIS: Where?
ROD: At thirty-eight Mintgum Crescent.
DENNIS: Huh?
ROD: You robbed your own house, dickhead.

ROD *pulls one from the pile and shows it to* DENNIS.

DENNIS: Is that mine?
ROD: It's Stavros' now. [*Running offstage, yelling*] Stavros! I've got a premium mat for you.

DENNIS *chases after.*

DENNIS: Fuck off I need that!

Jester

Liz Hobart

A square space. Flickering light from above – fluorescent lamps buzzing in a shopping arcade.

LEILA *enters, staring ahead at the centre of the space with a sense of recognition. The lights reach a steadiness, yet still threaten to flicker out at any moment.* LEILA *reaches the centre and whispers with a twitch of a smile.*

LEILA: You've really done it this time.

> *She checks that the coast is clear. She pulls out her phone.*
>
> SPARKY *shuffles in behind her, carrying a small bundle in a tea towel.* LEILA *does not look up from her phone.* SPARKY *pauses, watching* LEILA, *then tries to take a peek of what is inside the bundle.*

SPARKY: Kinda freaky, isn't she?

LEILA: Shh! Careful.

SPARKY: She can't hear me, she's all wrapped up!

LEILA: Well, if you don't keep your foghorn down, you'll wake up the whole bloody neighbourhood! It echoes, can't you tell?

> LEILA *puts her phone away.*

Here, let me take her.

> SPARKY *reluctantly starts passing over the bundle.*

SPARKY: Have you got her?

LEILA: Yep.

SPARKY: Are you sure?

LEILA: I think so…

> SPARKY *slowly releases the bundle. It nearly slips.*

Watch it!

SPARKY: But you said—

LEILA: I know, I know, it's just… you know, there's a lot of padding…

LEILA *gains a firmer hold. The pair stand in gentle silence, frozen, watching the bundle. Moving as one, the girls descend to a crouching position.* LEILA *lays the bundle down in the centre of the space.*

SPARKY: Not on the Jester's mouth!
LEILA: Why not?
SPARKY: Isn't that bad luck or something? I know it's just a picture but it looks like he's swallowing her up, doesn't it? Not very romantic.
LEILA: It's not meant to be romantic.
SPARKY: And why does it have to be in here anyway?
LEILA: You can think of somewhere better?

  SPARKY *tilts her head.*

SPARKY: The paint on his eyes is all worn off, it's all...
LEILA: It's perfect.
SPARKY: What about the park?
LEILA: I'm not putting roadkill in the fountain, Sparky. Let's be real. The Jester's face is right in the middle of the Arcade. Look at it. Smack bang centre of the cross.
SPARKY: My mum reckons it's actually a little off-centre, but—
LEILA: I don't care what your mum reckons. We don't care what anyone thinks, remember?
SPARKY: Nobody thinks about us at all.

  LEILA *repeatedly adjusts the position of the bundle.*

But I just think—

  LEILA *releases a heavy sigh.*

LEILA: Where do you want it, huh?
SPARKY: Hey!
LEILA: I'm sorry... I've just never done this before.
SPARKY: Obviously.
LEILA: But I've looked it all up, even on the dodgy sites. The Jester Arcade is perfect at this time of night. Shops are closed and no one comes through unless they're drunk.
  That's why I chose Tuesday. I need a centre point and I don't want Dad finding a chalk circle on the driveway... he'll think I've sold my soul or some shit.

SPARKY: And that's... not what this is?
LEILA: Of course not, it's an offering—I told you—
SPARKY: I know what you told me, Leila, but—
LEILA: But what?
SPARKY: Well, when's he getting here?
LEILA: Soon.
SPARKY: Aren't you nervous?
LEILA: Why should I be? We've been talking for a month and two days.
SPARKY: Do you know what he looks like?
LEILA: I'm not an idiot, you know.

>SPARKY *nods, thinking.*

SPARKY: Alright, what do we do next?

> *They hold eye contact for a moment.* LEILA *turns back to the bundle, a flash of uncertainty in her face that* SPARKY *does not catch.* LEILA *slowly unfolds each corner of the tea towel to reveal the corpse of a bird.*

Is she meant to be dead already?
LEILA: That's an optional part, I think.
SPARKY: But, you know... aren't you supposed to...

> SPARKY *tentatively mimes a violent act.*

Well, what did he tell you to do?
LEILA: He said I should do it myself.
SPARKY: Did you?!
LEILA: [*whispering*] Keep it down!
SPARKY: Leila!
LEILA: I found her in the gutter near the bakery. She got run over, I guess.
SPARKY: Are you gonna tell him?
LEILA: Tell him what?
SPARKY: Tell your boyfriend that you didn't follow the recipe.
LEILA: It's not a recipe, Sparky, Jesus.
SPARKY: Well, I don't know!
LEILA: He gave me guidelines...
SPARKY: He gave you instructions. He gave you rules. I thought you said you hated rules.

LEILA: Everyone says that. Plus it's not like that anyway. He said I didn't have to do it if I didn't want to. But this way I can show him I can be like him, I can be anything.

> LEILA *carefully slides the tea towel out from underneath the bird.* SPARKY *rubs her arms as a breeze passes through. She glances around, nervous.*

SPARKY: What if someone sees us?
LEILA: No-one's around.

> LEILA *begins splaying out one wing of the bird.*

SPARKY: What about your dad?
LEILA: He doesn't know I'm here. I turned off my location.
SPARKY: Won't that freak him out more?
LEILA: I'll say my phone died. He thinks I'm at yours.

> SPARKY *subtly pulls out her phone and switches off her own location.*

SPARKY: But what if he calls?
LEILA: I recorded a doco for him to watch. Something about guns. He'll get on the piss and pass out to it.

> SPARKY *is unconvinced.*

I promise.

> LEILA *starts splaying out the other wing.* SPARKY *leans in closer.*

SPARKY: She reminds me of my pet cockatiel.

> LEILA *closes her eyes to keep her patience.*

> SPARKY *awaits a response.*

> LEILA *continues with the bird.*

That one died too…

> LEILA *lets go of the bird and turns.*

LEILA: Look, if you don't want to be here, you can just… just—
SPARKY: I just think it's kinda messed up, alright? Dead birds aren't my thing…
LEILA: You don't have a thing, and that's worse. At least this can be mine.
SPARKY: Come on, Leila, it's not normal—
LEILA: Not everything has to be normal, can't you get that into your head?

SPARKY: All I know is that I wouldn't do all this for a guy I'd never even met!

Silence.

LEILA: What are you trying to say?
SPARKY: Nothing, I just—
LEILA: Spit it out!
SPARKY: Well… isn't he part of like a cult or something?

LEILA turns back to the bird, adjusting it.

LEILA: A community, it's different.
SPARKY: Sounds dodge to me.
LEILA: Well, it's not. It's actually pretty cool.
SPARKY: But you're not like… you're not gonna…
LEILA: I'll do whatever I damn want, Sparky!
SPARKY: What about me?!
LEILA: It's not about you!

SPARKY recoils slightly. She turns her nose up at LEILA, who holds the bird's wings with her fingertips.

SPARKY: You don't even know what you're doing, do you?

They stare at each other for a few moments.

LEILA turns back to the bird. She releases it, noticing the blood on the ends of her fingers.

She cradles the bird in her hands and slowly rises to her feet.

LEILA: It wasn't easy, Sparky. I had to scrape her body off the gravel. Her feathers were all stuck there with half-dried blood. I think she'd been run over more than once. I had to dodge a car at one point, peeling away her tail, trying to keep her in one piece—that's an important part. Ritual won't work otherwise. Can't offer a heart if it's broken, that kind of thing. But it was fiddly, because her guts were all… it was pretty rank, I'm not gonna lie. Still, I knew I was helping her. This poor little mess of wet feathers was gonna become something bigger than what she was meant for.

Pause.

I mean, I had to do it for him… you get it don't you? We talk online most nights now. That doesn't mean we're… you know… not yet.

I know I was meant to kill her myself, but I'll just have to tell him the truth later on. I'm scared that I might turn him off and he'll stop replying, and I'll just be back to nothing again...

Pause.

He says I can be whoever I want to be. I'm doing this for him—to prove that I can be my own person. I can be the girl who made a sacrifice in the Jester Arcade. Because who knows, maybe that is... me.

LEILA looks at the Jester on the floor for a moment, then at the bird. She smiles.

We should name her after the Jester. Makes sense, doesn't it? This'll be like a rebirth for her, trust me. I'm pretty sure it's a rebirth for me too.

Pause.

I guess it is a little romantic.

A sense of accomplishment washes over her as she holds the bird.

I've really done it this time.

SPARKY spots something ahead of LEILA. Her face fills with dread.

SPARKY: Leila!

LEILA does not respond.

Drop it, drop it now!

LEILA gently shakes her head.

It's a trick, Leila!

Suddenly, flashes go off from different sides of the square. Laughter, jeering, louder and louder.

LEILA frantically looks around, squinting as the flashes shine into her eyes. She instinctively pulls the bird towards her chest, protecting it.

SPARKY moves around LEILA, attempting to shield her from the cameras. LEILA holds the bird tighter. She closes her eyes.

The Witch in the Window
Alexander Lee-Rekers

BEC *makes her way down the staircase of an abandoned house; she sits on the bottom step and digs a handful of long rusty nails out of her pocket, which she leaves in a pile by her side. A long, slow, deep breath in and out.*

SARAH *enters through the front door with a bulging satchel slung over her shoulder. She hopscotches over uneven flooring to* BEC *and sits down, heaving the satchel onto her lap.*

BEC: Chips?

SARAH: A feast.

BEC: But you brought chips, right?

> SARAH *pulls a plastic bag full of snacks out of the satchel and empties its contents onto the floor.*

SARAH: Starches, jellies, sours, chocolate… All the food groups.

> BEC *picks up a chip packet and squeezes it a little.* SARAH *picks up one of the nails and turns it over in her hands.*

Are you all right?

BEC: Remember being scared of this house when you were little?

SARAH: I—yeah?

BEC: Remember why?

SARAH: Why? I just was. We just were.

BEC: My sister told me a family died here. The father went berserk and shot his wife and kids and then threw himself down the stairs.

SARAH: That is classic 'your sister'.

BEC: Once, I realised that if I climbed the fence into the nature reserve behind my backyard, I could cut straight through to this property—down by the creek bed. I did it one time after school: I got here just as the sun was going down, and I looked up at this house… and the way the sun shone through the cracks and gaps in the walls made it look like it was glowing, like it was alive.

Pause.

I kept thinking, as I walked home through the bush, that any second I'd turn around and see—

SARAH *lets the nail clunk to the floor.* BEC *jumps.*

—something following me.

SARAH: You mean… the house?

She half-giggles at the thought.

Sneaking up on you? And then ducking behind a tree every time you turn around and look back?

Nothing from BEC. SARAH *starts on a chocolate bar.*

BEC: I hate kids.

SARAH: [*chewing slowly*] You are a kid.

BEC: No, like little kids. The loud, sticky kind. They're, like, the price I pay for twenty dollars an hour and dinner in the oven and Foxtel.

SARAH: Babysitting's a hella cushy gig, though. Try making popcorn at Hoyts…

BEC: But it's not 'hella cushy', Sarah, it's hard. 'Cause the things that make parents trust me and want to hire me actually make me bad at the job. Kids don't care about you being responsible or sensible. They don't care about dinner or bedtime, they just want you to be fun or let them stay up late.

SARAH: You're fun.

BEC: It doesn't matter. Because I hate kids. I don't enjoy babysitting, I just get the job done.

The sound of a siren out on the road. SARAH *tears open a packet of gummy worms as* BEC *watches on.*

BEC: You're drunk, aren't you…

SARAH: Yeah. Yeah okay, look: I was at a party when you messaged and I'm a little 'sozzled' as my dad says. But it worked out: when I got your message to bring snacks I went into the kitchen and raided the pantry. Didn't you hate it when people started throwing 'grown-up' parties with alcohol and felt like they couldn't put bowls of lollies out anymore?

BEC: I want you to help me burn this house down.

SARAH: I'm sorry?

BEC: I looked up the best way to start a fire and the internet says a chip packet because the oil burns hot and they can't tell it's arson—
SARAH: Why do you want to burn this house down?
BEC: I hurt Benny— I hurt Benny Parsons tonight. Badly.

The siren on the road begins again and they listen to it until it fades away.

Babysitting is all about fear. You've gotta be all 'I'll tell your parents', but that only works for a while because they realise you're not telling on them every time and call your bluff. You gotta get the fear back; find new ways to scare. So.
SARAH: So?
BEC: I created a monster. A witch. She lives right here, in this old house on the hill. Nobody's seen her for years and years… but she's seen you. 'You don't believe me?' I'd say. 'Look for her in the window on your way to school.' And you might not see her, or her white hair, or her dark red eyes, but you'll see the curtains flutter when she steps back into shadow. Or maybe her figure in silhouette against the sunset. She preys on kids that misbehave. They'd go: 'That's stupid, Bec. Why does she care if I'm good or not?' And I'd lean in, give them my debate-team-captain smile and say: 'Because she knows you won't be missed.'
SARAH: Wow.
BEC: She wasn't perfect, because unlike parents she can't turn up at the end of the night. But I made sure there was plenty to draw from. The house, nursery rhymes I'd make up, stories about missing pets and claw-marks on trees in the nature reserve. And she does this thing where she 'marks' you: she sneaks into your room and leaves you a token, a warning.

BEC picks up one of the nails from the pile.

From the floorboards. Straight from the floorboards to under the pillow. Here.

She hands it to SARAH.

So be good.
SARAH: What happened with Benny?
BEC: Benny Parsons is the biggest… little shit I look after. His parents drop him off at mine—they're out of town tonight, so he's staying

over. It's dinner... and I feed him fish fingers and put on *Finding Nemo*. The combo didn't sit right.

> BEC *almost laughs as she thinks back on this.* SARAH *has stopped eating.*

He's screaming and he's pounding his fists on the coffee table and I'm sitting there, calm, because I know as soon as I mention the witch he'll settle. But not tonight. 'There's no such thing. My dad said so!' And then he threatens me: says he's going to walk home to his house and sit on his front step all night, and when his parents get back in the morning tell them how I like to scare all the kids in town and I'm no fun. 'The witch'll get you, Benny.' 'There's no. Such. Thing.' He sniffs up his tears and walks out the door.

> SARAH *holds out some chocolate.* BEC *takes a square and nibbles the corner.*

I run out to my backyard and I jump the fence into the reserve. I cut across the creek bed, sprint up the hill and I let myself in here. I wait upstairs by a window... Benny's wandering down the road, like even though there's only one street you can take between my house and his, he's worried about getting lost. And I'm a good hundred metres away—can't even see his face—but I can tell: he's scared of the witch. I step up to the window. I feel the sunset hit me from behind. And I point at him and scream.

> *Silence.*

Benny jolts like someone grabbed his neck and shook his spine. He does this weird kinda dance that looks like he doesn't know whether to race back to my house or continue on to his. And so he's twisting on the spot when the car reaches the crest and sees him and hits its brakes and for such a small body, for such a little person, the thud was so loud, Sarah. It was so real.

> SARAH *sways, like she's only just feeling the alcohol hit.*

SARAH: You want to burn down the witch's house?

BEC: I loved the idea of being grown up, you know? And I'm not. To anybody. Not to parents, not to kids. All of the burden and none of the respect and that middle ground is really hurting me. I think I killed Benny.

SARAH: No, you didn't.
BEC: Oh my God I killed a kid, a little boy…
SARAH: He's going to be okay.

> BEC *stares at the mess of snacks at her feet. Then she clocks something in their midst, and picks up a receipt.*

BEC: I thought you stole these from a party?

> *Pause.*

SARAH: The pantry was really healthy—
BEC: But these are from—you had time to shop and then double back here?
SARAH: My dad picked me up.
BEC: Your dad knows we're here?

> SARAH'*s phone vibrates. She looks down at the message and back to* BEC.

SARAH: Everybody does. It's okay. Benny's going to be okay. They just need you to come down and talk to them.
BEC: Am I in trouble?
SARAH: I don't think so. They didn't say that. You're a kid.

> BEC *nods.* SARAH *squeezes her hand.*

We're down by the road. He's going to be fine.
BEC: Okay. Thanks.

> SARAH *exits.* BEC *looks around the room one more time; up to the staircase. She reaches down, picks up a single nail and slips it into her pocket.*

Bin Chicken

Madelaine Nunn

Luke's gender can be changed. Character names can be changed to suit the diversity of the cast.

Friday night. 10 pm. Large cubes of compressed plastic bottles are stacked high around the outskirts of a tall mound of recyclable rubbish. Timber, tyres and discarded bric-a-brac line the surface, hiding years of rubbish underneath. Next to the tip is a recycle shop that doubles as a house out the back. This is KATY*'s house.*

KATY *is standing on top of the mound with a backpack on. She paces back and forth looking into the distance while using an industrial-sized torch to inspect the area below. On the other side of the mound is* LUKE, KATY*'s boyfriend. He stands still with his torch fixed in position; he is also keeping a lookout but has less intensity than* KATY.

At the base of the tip there is a sign that reads: 'We're here and we're here to stay. We won't give up, we won't give in'.

LUKE: If you keep shining the torch like that they're going to know we're up here.

KATY: Good, I want them to know we're up here.

LUKE: When you asked me to do a stake-out I was picturing eating doughnuts in the front seat of my car, not standing in the dark with torches on top of your tip.

KATY: I want them to know that I'm ready for them this time. The best offence is a strong defence, I've always said that.

LUKE: I've never heard you say that.

KATY: Well, I've always thought it.

LUKE: Could you at least stop pacing around, it doesn't seem safe.

KATY: Are you scared?

LUKE: What? No! It's the structure of this thing, it's an avalanche waiting to happen.

KATY: That's a new one.

LUKE: I'm just saying, what if it collapses and we get trapped and have to cut each other's arms off, like that rock climber guy.

KATY: Don't worry, I have a Stanley knife in my backpack.

LUKE: Why do you have a Stanley knife in your backpack?

KATY: Just in case this thing collapses and I have to cut my own arm off.

LUKE: Be honest, if you had to, would you do it?

KATY: It's not going to collapse! Are you keeping watch on your side or not?

LUKE: Don't worry, no trespassers yet. There's been one ute on the south road in the last ten minutes, your parents are still safely watching TV in the lounge room and the security light hasn't been on since Pilot went out the dog door.

KATY: Good, I'm glad you're being thorough.

LUKE: As a reward can you stop patrolling for a second and admire the view with me? It's actually not so bad here at night.

KATY: Less of an eyesore?

LUKE: I didn't mean—I mean, you can see the whole town from up here.

KATY: You only just realising how big your house is.

LUKE: No. I've just never seen the town from this angle before, in a weird way it's actually, kind of… beautiful.

KATY: Really?

LUKE: Once you get used to the smell.

KATY: Just keep a lookout, would you. I don't want any of those douchebags vandalising the shop again.

LUKE: Yes ma'am.

KATY: Don't call me ma'am.

LUKE: Stop acting like a ma'am then.

KATY: I'm not acting like a ma'am.

LUKE: I thought this was meant to be fun.

KATY: Why would it be fun?

LUKE: I don't know.

KATY opens her backpack and chucks him a fedora.

KATY: Here, have this hat, hats are fun.

LUKE: I'm only wearing it if it makes me look adorable and handsome at the same time.

He puts on the hat and presents himself to KATY *but goes unnoticed as she continues to explore the area below.*

So?

KATY: What?

LUKE: Does it make me look adorable and handsome at the same time?

KATY *turns to look at him.*

KATY: Oh God! You look exactly like Mr Dallis at the swimming carnival!

LUKE: [*impersonating Mr Dallis' deep voice*] 'Girls and boys! Contrary to popular belief, participation in the swimming carnival is compulsory, not voluntary. I repeat compulsory. I want to see every single one of you wet by the end of the day.'

KATY: He's such a ped.

LUKE: Defs a ped. Where did you get this hat from?

KATY: I found it on the ground on the way up here.

LUKE: What?!

LUKE *rips the hat off and chucks it on the ground.*

Eww. Why would you—I had that on my head, probably had lice or rabies or who-knows-what infested in it.

KATY: Jeez, it's just a hat.

LUKE: Why would you pick it up?

KATY: It looked expensive so I was going to give it to Mum to sell in the shop.

LUKE: You could've warned me before I put it on my head.

KATY: If you're so disgusted by this place then maybe you shouldn't have come.

LUKE: I'm not saying—

KATY: What? We both know you can't stand it on this side of town.

LUKE: Well it's not exactly how I wanted to spend my Friday night.

KATY: It's not exactly how I wanted to spend my night either.

LUKE: …

KATY: What?

LUKE: Nothing.

KATY: Tell me.

LUKE: You're better than this! I hate to say it, because I know your parents are having a tough time but no matter how much they protest the tip's probably going to get shut down. And to be honest, and don't hate me for saying this, I think it's actually a good thing. You can start afresh and finally stop being known as the recycle centre chick—

KATY: The tip chick, the recycle dyke, the trash rash or my personal favourite, the bin chicken—

LUKE: You shouldn't listen to that—

KATY: I'm only called those things because your mate Darcy came up with them and don't talk about my parents when you don't know shit.

LUKE: Katy I'm trying to help you. You said it yourself, you hate this place, you were always complaining about having to work here.

KATY: Everyone complains about their crap part-time job. I live where I work, and where I work is a tip, and my parents are my boss—

LUKE: You voted at the meeting! You said you were glad there was finally a lobby group to shut this place down, you specifically said, 'Thank fuck, I'll wear that shirt'—

KATY: I was stupid okay! If I could take my vote back I would, I'd take it back a thousand times. I didn't think people would start trying to destroy the place when my parents put up a fight, I didn't realise people would turn so ugly.

LUKE: It's ugly now, but think about the future.

KATY: I am!

LUKE: You know as well as I do this tip was bringing us all down, the trucks and the types of people it was attracting to the town—

KATY: Is that the excuse your mum and all her salon friends use?

LUKE: My mum has never cared that you live here—

KATY: Does she give everyone hand sanitiser and make them leave their shoes at the door?

LUKE: That's just—

KATY: Let's not forget when Darcy and your friends spray-painted Dad's car, and yeah, don't think I didn't know it was them.

LUKE: That was shit, everything everyone has done has been shit. You didn't deserve that. But when this whole things blows over, and the people get what they want everything will go back to normal—

KATY: You don't get it! It's never been normal for me! I've always been different. Since I can remember everyone has always made jokes,

jokes that I never thought were funny but I laughed anyway because what else was I meant to do. But this is my home, this is where I grew up, this is who I am. I'd rather be a bin chicken than to go on pretending like I don't care. How do you think my parents got the money to send me to your school in the first place? If the tip shuts I'll be put straight into Crescent High and then what? Will you still talk to me? Still have me round for dinner? Still invite me to your parties? So, if you'd rather be at Darcy's plotting ways to take my family down then go. But I'll be here all night every night if I have to.

Beat.

LUKE *picks up the fedora and holds it in his hand.*

LUKE: I'm sorry.

Slight pause.

I was a douche, I was a big douche and I'm sorry. I don't want to go to Darcy's, I don't want to go anywhere, I just want to be with you and if you're going to be here all night every night then I'll be here all night every night. Except Tuesday night, I have that Bio exam the next day, but every day, other than that day, I'll be here with you keeping guard!

He puts on the fedora.

Slight pause.

KATY: Thanks.

A crashing is heard. They both jolt, take out their torches and point them to the left.

Who's there?

LUKE: Come out you cowards!

Another rustling is heard to the right. In synchronisation they quickly turn their torches.

Oi! Come out!

LUKE *slowly steps towards the noise.* KATY *stays back with her torch scanning around.*

LUKE: Oh my god!
KATY: What!?

LUKE: It's one of those—
KATY: What!?
LUKE: Grim reaper birds!
KATY: What?
   A squawking is heard.
It's a, it's a bin chicken!

Victoria's Secret Angel Virgin / Bakerz Delight
Julia Rorke

JESS, *17, stands on stage in a tight black dress with her shoes sitting next to her. She is in front of a mirror looking at herself, she is holding her phone in her hand.*

This piece's text messages can be read by the actor playing JESS *or they could be done as a voiceover, funky audio-visual effect, etc.*

The phone vibrates. JESS *looks at it.*

JESS: 'Ten minutes.'

>*She breathes in and out a bit over-dramatically, and then starts to hurriedly throw make-up on, fucking up her eyeliner.*

Shit, shit, shit.

>*She starts redoing it.*

I'm meeting Tom, this guy—I met him when I was working at Hoyts last summer. It was shit because they barely let you watch any free movies at all, which was why I wanted to work there in the first place, well that and also because I needed a different job to the one I had the summer before. So the summer before I gained heaps of weight working at Bakers Delight, like it was my mum who told me I should quit, because of how many white chocolate and blueberry scones I was eating. No but wait, you don't understand, at the end of every single day they would chuck literally everything leftover out! Like I mean everything, all of it! They couldn't even give it away to the homeless because apparently there are laws against that like O.H. and S. bullshit because in case the homeless people sue them in case they get sick, like, as if the homeless people even have enough money to sue Bakers Delight if the bread's off and they get sick, that's why they're homeless you fucking idiots, anyway so they would chuck it all out and just make all new shit the next morning, and there was always sooooooooo much left over and food waste gives me anxiety so I would take home as much stuff as I could, like, I would legit fill three garbage bags with bread, cheese-and-Vegemite scrolls, finger buns, et cetera, et cetera, you know what I mean, you've been to Bakers Delight, and I would always just eat heaps when I was there as well, and Mum got pissed off because she said my skin was getting really shit again and the money she was spending on me going to the naturopath to make it better was just going to waste, but yeah, anyway, it was pretty fun working with Tom… at Hoyts, I mean…

Anyway I'm supposed to be meeting him at the pub down the road in ten minutes…

And I know he's going to want to have sex with me tonight, because we've already hooked up twice without doing it so I just know that that's what the deal is for tonight.

I've never even put anything up there before, like I myself haven't even been up there, so honestly… I don't even know…

Both times before he's said that I'd given him 'blue balls' because I wouldn't do anything to him—ew, but anyway I just don't reckon he would be coming all the way here tonight if he didn't think we were going to do it…

She starts straightening her hair hurriedly.

I do think he legit likes me though… I dunno… part of me realllllllly wants to, part of me thinks I have to and part of me thinks maybe I don't want to because of the fact that maybe he expects me to, that sort of makes me not want to, but then I do want to… like, I feel like I'm on fire when I'm around him. I've never felt that before except with Joel Thompson but that was back when I was like seven to thirteen and I had approx six conversations with him in those entire six years. Tom's the first guy I've liked with that I've actually known, and I think he likes me back…

Phone vibrates again.

'Hey I'm five minutes away.'

Aghhhhhh fuck he's almost here, fuck, fuck, fuck I'm gonna vomitttt!

She gets out a bottle of vodka from her cupboard and has a shot.

Erghhh.

[*Accusingly*] What?

But maybe I shouldn't even care if he expects us to have sex though? Like most guys who are his age, would I think, because I suppose girls his age are way more relaxed about it... and experienced... maybe it's just me being weird, why does he like me then? If I'm weird?

But anyway whatever, why am I even nervous? I'm hotter than him anyway! No like, he's hot, I definitely think he's hot, obviously, I mean I like him heaps, I like him a lot, except I hate what he wears, what he wears makes me want to throw up, like baggy jeans and skater shoes and yellow tops—

Like it literally makes me want to throw up a bit in my mouth when I see him—

Like I almost hate him a bit when I see him.

But then it's like I think about him and everything he's ever said to me, for approx twelve hours out of the twenty-four hours in a day, and that's actually a lot considering I'm asleep for ten hours out of the day and the other two hours I'm thinking about whether it's weird I need to go to the toilet again since it's only been thirty minutes since I last peed or yelling at dumb bitches who I think are holding our modern history class back, they're like:

'LOL did Hitler invade Laos?'

'NO YOU FUCKING IDIOT THAT'S POL POT!'

'Haha WHATEVARRRRR chill out Jess you psychooo have a fucking durry we're not even getting ATARs anywayyyyy.'

'Well why the fuck are you here then??? Go and start your TAFE degree in personal training tomorrow instead you idiots.'

Derroez.

   Pause.

It's hard though because I can't really tell any of my friends about him. He's not like the boys the girls I hang with at school are friends with, he's not like them at all actually... I don't know, around Tom I actually feel like a person. The first time we hooked up was at the Hoyts staff party at the very end of the night and the second time was when he met up with me when I was out with some friends—but I didn't want them to know I was meeting up with him or anything, so I ghosted them and went and met him out the front of the club and we went somewhere else.

We were walking down the street toward the other bar and he jokingly asks, 'You look really nice, are you wearing that for me?'

I was wearing a tight black dress and chunky black wedges—no, a different dress to this tight black dress, this one has ruffles, see, but same shoes—anyway, I felt really awkward and didn't know what to say so I just acted like I didn't hear him.

Phone vibrates again.

'Hey which pub again? I just got off the bus. Be a few minutes.'

Ah shit he's thereeee! Fuckkkkkk thisssss blah NAAAHHHHHH I don't even want to go anymore I'm just gonna put my pyjamas back on and go to sleep and just not talk to him anymore.

He'll be like, 'What happened to her?' and I'll be like, 'Soz, I'm dead.' We can just do it in heaven instead, when I'm an angel virgin and nothing you stick inside of me is going to hurt and I'll be a freaky Victoria's Secret Sex Chick who totez has heaps of freaky sex skillzzzzzzzz.

She has another shot.

What if I'm a virgin forever but?

I don't want to leave it too late so it gets to that awkward stage where it's not 'cute' that I haven't had sex yet but just weird and guys will think there's something wrong with me and then I'll have to stick a carrot or something up there or like get a guy that I'm friends with to just have sex with me to get it out of the way so I'm not a massive freak except that's not gonna work either because I don't have guy friends, cuz I'm such a weirdo and I'm not able to think about guys except in relation to whether I wanna hook up with them or not and then I get nervous that they can read my mind and can tell I'm thinking about whether I want to hook up with them or not and then I can't talk to them.

Especially not the guys the girls at school are friends with, all they give a shit about is surfing and doughnuts and they're rank, maybe they wear cool shit but they're such assholes and the girls just do whatever they want them to do it's so fucking rank.

Phone vibrates again.

'Hello?'

I don't think I can go actually—the second time we hooked up we went back to his house and I lay in bed next to him, but turned away from him, I was still wearing my bra and undies. He tried to ramp up the mood a bit, by being cute, complimenting my body and shit, he ran his finger over the curve of my waist and hip, but I still didn't know what to say, I legit couldn't even talk or look at him. I think after a bit I kind of just started blabbing on about this guy who had been chatting me up at my new weekend job at the tennis centre, I didn't say whether or not I liked the tennis guy back or anything, I didn't like the tennis guy by the way, he was really lame and gross actually, but HAH—I just thought that seemed like an appropriate point of conversation to bring up at the time… goddddddd I'M SO STUPID! Well, I didn't know what else to say! And then I said I was at the end of my period so I couldn't do anything, and then he said I couldn't get pregnant at the end of my period…

Phone vibrates again.

'Hey where are you?'

She picks up her chunky black shoes and looks at her phone for ten seconds. Bites her fingernails or something.

Phone vibrates again.

'Hey I've been waiting for ages now, are you still coming?'

Umm…

She puts her shoes on, looks at herself in the mirror again, flips her hair and walks off the stage.

Get Gone
David Stewart

1.
Out the back of Woolworths.
- This town is toxic.
- This town is rank.
- This town is nasty and toxic and rank.
- So nasty and toxic and rank.
- Smells like piss.
- Three-week-old piss.
- It's so tragic.
- What an eyesore.
- Nothing to do here.
- Nothing to see.
- Just a whole lotta nothing.
- It's got a CocoBliss but?
- And a Goodlife?
- Nah. Burn em ay!
- Down to the ground
- Time to go.
- Gotta get out.
- Gotta get gone.

2.
Out the back of Woolworths.
- Ever wonder what we look like?
- Huh?
- You mean us?

– Nah. The town.
– From up there. Bird's eye.
– How far up?
– Beyond the clouds?
– In space?
– From Pluto?
– From another galaxy?
– Yeah, but like, imagine you're looking through an intergalactic telescope of some alien race.
– Down on us.
– Right now.
– On our smoko.
– Out the back of Woolies.
– What do we look like?
– Dunno.
– Haven't thought really.
– Cousin's an astronaut. Could ask?
– Want a medal?
– Err ya fag.
– Can't say that.
– Says who?
– Miss Kerrigan.
– Why not?
– Cuz it's not PC.
– Shut ya mouth, PC Nazi!
– Gonna eff you up.
– Go on then.
– Do it ya hero!
– Could ask him?
– Could do.
– Be lit to know.

– Imagine being up there now.
– Floating.
– In orbit.
– Not a care in the world.
– Not chained to anything.
– Free from all the sh—
– Lookin' down.
– See the curve of the mountain?
– Beyond the broadcast station.
– It's bending round, semi-circle.
– Like a horseshoe.
– A horseshoe!
– That's what it looks like!
– Nah. Ten bucks says an Ender Portal.
– Put twenty on a fidget spinner.
– As if. You're screwed brah!
– That twenty's mine.
– Nah. Fiddy bucks says a bloated arsehole.
– Be serious!
– So am, just Google Mapsed it ay.
– Show us then!
– Prove it.
– Chuck us ya phone!
– You don't believe huh?
– You're a serial liar!
– Fine. Read it and weep suck-azzzzzz.
– Holy shit.
– Can't believe it.
– Does too.
– You were right.
– Looks like a prolapsed arse.

– We really do.
– Live on a shit hole.
– We really do.
– Live in a goatse.
– Fuckin' swell. 'Welcome to the crack of the East Coast.'
– Gotta get out now.
– Need a plan first.
– True dat!
– Time's a-tickin'.
– Gotta get gone.

3.
The aisles of Woolworths.
- Lady mumbles over the speaker.
- 'Could I get a price check on psyllium husk, a price check on psyllium husk?'
- Silly what?
- Psyllium.
- What's that?
- Overpriced fibre for yuppies.
- Total rip job if you ask us.
- Screw this!
- Not paid enough for this crap.
- Not got the time for this crap.
- Not got the energy for this crap.
- What a waste of life.
- Gotta to be something better.
- Greener pastures.
- Something better than.
- Serve.
- Beep.

– Stock.
– Repeat.
– Serve.
– Beep.
– Stock.
– Gluten-free pasta.
– Alkalised water.
– Spirulina.
– Macadamia milk.
– That from the nips of macadamias?
– Kale.
– Activated almonds.
– Organic blueberries.
– Seven dollars a punnet.
– Why we got all this crap again? It's a total rort!
– Cause the town's got fancy.
– Ever since the tourist boom.
– Ever since we got gentrified.
– That the word?
– Yeah.
– Burn it down.
– Fire sale.
– What do you get if you burn down Woolies?
– What?
– Coles.
– Lady calls over the loudspeaker.
– 'Clean-up on aisle three, that's clean-up on aisle three.'
– That's our lane!
– What's she mean?
– Does she mean us?
– Are we the spill?

– Hope not.
– Maybe we are?
– We're waiting.
– Who's gonna sop us up?
– No-one comes.
– We're waiting.
– Who's gonna sop us up?
– … anyone?

4.

Out the front of Woolworths.

– Broke its neck.
– On impact.
– You reckon?
– Say so.
– What happened?
– Just look up.
– They're dropping like rain.
– All morning.
– Jesus!
– Poor little things.
– Tweet tweet.
– Little birdies.
– There's another inside.
– Fell through the skylight.
– Head first into the prune juice.
– Told ya that shit could kill ya.
– This one's still twitching, see?
– Don't poke it.
– Can't look.
– Nothing we can do.

– Just gotta watch until he—
– …
– Poor bastard.
– What a way to go.
– Look, you can practically see its vertebrae!
– Shut up! Have some respect!
– But legit, it's like a real fucked-up pop-up book.
– You reckon Valencia or Amaro?
– Don't film it!
– No, do.
– This shit don't happen every day!
– Keep that camera rolling baby!
– There's more falling. See!
– One.
– Two.
– Three.
– Splat.
– Hoah! Shit!
– Did you see that one?
– Jesus. He kamikazied the fuck outta that windshield!
– Left a hefty dint!
– Fat Terry won't be happy 'bout that!
– What is even happening!
– It's an event!
– Like… what… the apocalypse?
– Are we gonna get raptured up?
– Wait a sec. Maybe we did this?
– Nah, it's this place isn't it.
– It's toxic.
– It's rank.
– It's nasty and toxic and rank.

– Quit bagging it.
– So negative all the time.
– Don't need that energy.
– You can't deny, it's got something.
– Something special.
– It's ours.
– It's our—
– We shouldn't be ashamed of where we come from!
– But gots a—
– What?
– Gots this empty feeling.
– Craving.
– Grabbing my insides.
– For something larger.
– Greater.
– Than ourselves.
– A desire for—
– Don't know how to—
– Can't explain—
– Just can't help feeling I'm better than this, you know?
– Like I'm expected to be something.
– More.
– Like I'm simply not…
– Like what I am is not…
– Enough.
– …
– Don't wanna go.
– Not sure we're ready.
– But we need to.
– Make something of ourselves.
– Be something.

– It's expected.
– Yeah.
– S'pose you're right.
– Gotta get out now.
– Gotta get a plan.
– Yeah, guess it's time to get gone...
– ... Someone should probably bin it ay...
– Yeah... probably.
– Don't look at me! I'm not gonna touch it!
– Fine. I'm getting the tongs.

5.
Back office of Woolworths.
– Reckon this'll work?
– Dude, YouTube's where it's at.
– It's the only way.
– To get rich quick.
– Or die trying.
– Do people really want to see this stuff?
– Chhhyeah!
– People dig this kinda content.
– Everyone's a little fucked up.
– Everyone's got a fetish.
– People get off on bursting pimples.
– Sites like Mr Zit get hectic traffic!
– But how much more epic is this?
– Dead birds pissing from the sky!
– It's some 'nek level' David Attenborough shit!
– Alright! Uploading now.
– Sick.
– Holy shit!

– What's taking so long?
– Can't wait much longer!
– I want it now!
– Just be patient!
– It's the shoddy connection here.
– NBN. More like NBF!
– National Broadband Fuckaround.
– Okay. Here we go.
– We're active baby!
– …
– Anything yet?
– Nothing so far?
– Just be patient!
– I am!
– Can you speed it up?
– Wait a sec.
– What?
– We got our first view.
– YAAAAAAS QWEEN!
– I count a hundred now.
– A thousand.
– Ten thousand.
– One hundred thousand.
– Holy shit.
– This is whack.
– Are we trending?
– Think so.
– We've gone viral baby!
– Man the phones!
– Wait for the call.
– What call?

- The call!
- From who?
- Producers.
- YouTube.
- Fucking Ellen.
- Any bugger who wants to sign us!
- We've got a hit!
- Can't believe this!
- This is it!
- We're actually gonna make it!
- Put this place on the map.
- Be… a… a… something!
- Can you imagine?
- Us?
- Stars of all the Cons!
- Sell-out international tour.
- Stretch hummers.
- Luxury hotels.
- I'm pretty much jizzing with joy.
- Are you ready?
- So amped!
- Hashtag celeb-lyf!
- We're gonna be rolling in all da coins!
- Move over Queen B.
- Move over PewDiePie.
- Move over Kimmy K.
- Move over Meghan Trainor.
- Oh, nah, she's dirt ay.
- Nah, yeah, she's dirt.
- Can't believe—
- We're gonna get gone!

– No, really!
– Can't believe we're really really really gonna get the fuck gone!
– It feels so right.
– It feels soo—
– I know.
– The time couldn't be more perfect!
– Our time is—
– Lady mumbles over the loud speaker.
– 'Still waiting on that price check. Psyllium husk price check. Thank you.'
– …
– Maybe now's not the…
– Yeah…
– Don't blow ya wad too soon you know?
– We're still young.
– Dumb.
– Full of—
– Dreaming hurt no-one though.
– True…
– S'pose we should make the most of this then.
– We got time on our side…
– Yeah!
– You're right!
– This is our home!
– This is our destiny!
– This is our shithole!
– Yeah!
– Dream later.
– Don't strike the match.
– Enjoy the rank while it lasts.

Snap to black.

Cul-de-sac

Phoebe Sullivan

High school car park. Late afternoon. WOMAN *stands, waiting.*

WOMAN: Cul-de-sac.

   Pause.

   Cull… Kill…

   Kill-de-sack?

   Pause.

   Cull-the-sack! Hah, yeah.

   I love words.

   Cul-de-sac is an interesting word, but not a great design for a school car park.

   The plural for cul-de-sac, believe it or not, is not cul-de-sacs. The plural for cul-de-sac is culs-de-sac. It's French, and that's all Mr Cramp had to say about that. There are two culs-de-sac at my school. I'm waiting at one of them.

   For Dad.

   I'm waiting for my dad.

   Right now I'm reading this book. It's kind of shit. Well, not shit, presumptuous more than anything. The author's written about this main dude who is meant to be this soul-searching, outlaw-on-the-run who, I imagine, I'm supposed to care about. And like, sure, there are some parts where I go, 'Awh, that's nice'. But, and I think this is where he, the writer, stuffs up because there are so many other parts where his character, Rooney-something, is just… an awful person. Like this terrible, awful, and right now I keep trying to, I keep asking: Why? Why should I care about anything that happens to this man? I hate him.

   I dunno.

   We have to read it for school, so I'm trying not to get too involved.

So this guy's just murdered some woman, in the book, again, and I'm sitting here thinking 'Why?', and I look up from my book because maybe a reasonable answer has driven itself into the car park. One of the two cul-de-sacs. Culs-de-sac. Shit.

It hasn't though.

But I do see Ratna. Mrs V, actually, but she lets me call her Ratna because of a joke I made in her class where I said I was her favourite, to which she agreed and now I call her by her first name. She left school a while ago to have her baby, which she also has with her now.

Mr Cramp, whose first name I might add is Richard—

Pause.

Richard Cramp.

Pause.

Let that sink in.

Pause.

Mr Cramp is relieving Ratna's English class while she's on maternity leave. It also happens to be my English class. The reason I have to read this glorified toilet paper, trash pile.

I see Ratna with her baby strapped to her front, her mouth resting on the top of its head like she's in the middle of kissing it, only she just stays like that, frozen. Or, if she does move, she'll gently shake her head side to side, brushing her lips against the soft hairs.

Pause.

Sometimes I think about what it'd be like if I had a baby.

Not like, now, obviously. I don't want a baby right now. Gross!

But, you know, even if you don't want one you can think about it. Which, I do. Sometimes... They just look so soft. Their tiny hands. Their cute little, squishy, always grasping-for-things hands. And the way they hold onto your finger with their entire, well, you know, classic baby photo stuff.

And I love how baby clothes are just mini versions of adult clothes! Which

Like

Yeah

Obviously.

But I never really thought about it properly until Mum and I were in Myers and we walked from the men's section to the women's section, which meant we had to pass through the baby section, and there were these men's chinos that were exactly the same as a pair of pants in the baby section. And I was like:

Mum!

Mum!

MUM!

These chinos, right? See these chinos? See them?

Now, look at these!

Holds up baby pants.

Mum, look. Look! LOOK!

These chinos are exactly the same as man chinos, but they're baby chinos!

Baby. Chinos.

Pause.

Mum?

Pause.

You know when you finally catch yourself daydreaming and you have no idea how much time has passed? Well, it's been long enough for Ratna to notice me staring, her slightly concerned eyes trying to catch my attention. Probably to get me to stop creeping on her and her baby. Which I do, like, immediately.

That's when I first see the car. This shiny black convertible, exiting the roundabout, rolling into the school car park.

Pause.

Porsche. Fancy.

Katrin's uncle used to own a Jag which was this disgusting green colour. Racing Green, apparently. It's an old people colour. The way that rum-and-raisin is an old people icecream flavour, which is also disgusting. Anyway, Katrin's uncle's car ended up being repossessed because of credit fraud and that was a few years ago, so I have no idea who'd own a sports car in this part of town anymore.

I wait for it to drive past, but it doesn't.

It parks right in front of me, engine still running, and then... Nothing.

I look around. None of the kids left walk towards the car.

A horn beeps.

Me?

I stand up and walk over to the car. Its tinted glass means I only see my reflection. If my reflection was an inky, distorted blob.

'Vvv'.

That's the sound of the car window being wound down.

'Vvvvvvvvvv'.

Slowly, my tar-monster head is erased and I can see the driver inside.

Pause.

You know how in some B-grade action films, right at the climax, the protagonist finds out something pivotal about their past which prevents them from being able to save the day? The action usually takes place somewhere like a sinking ship or an abandoned warehouse on the verge of collapse, symbolic of the character's emotions in disarray.

There's the sound of explosives going off, sirens, shooting, all muffled by this head-splitting ringing. As the hero stumbles out of the wreckage, blood streaming from their forehead, we see a close-up of their face as they look to the sky. They didn't ask for this! What does it all mean? Out of nowhere clouds gather and heavy rain starts to pour, a thousand violins play, our hero falls to their knees, lighting SFX, throws back their head, camera pedestals upward, and screams: 'Why?'

'WHHHHHHYYYYY!'

Pause.

That's not exactly what's happening right now, but it's pretty close.

And also why I'm Ratna's favourite.
Pause.
I don't really… What do I say?
There's Dad. Sitting in the car. This shiny black Porsche. Giant grin smacked on his face saying, 'Look what I've got!' And then Mum in my head, softly stifling tears in the bathroom, one of my ears pressed against the door trying to hear her conversation to the bank.
I don't…
I don't want to. I know it's there, his side to everything, but I don't want to have to understand. I'm way too… Okay, sure, there's clearly some form of love here.
He buys a Porsche
And it's
It's
Exciting
And he's excited about being able to share this really beautiful car with me
And it is
Yeah
Nice
If I wasn't so fucking
Shiny
My reflection
It is a really nice, shiny, black, expensive
Mum
There's Mum
Still
His big stupid smile
So happy
He doesn't know
Cul-de-sac
It's not that bad.

But

I know

He knows

You can't just

In spite of everything, I know he knows that in some way he's failed. Like, deep down he's aware of it. He sees me sitting at the table, eating soggy fish and chips for dinner, wishing I was with Mum, and I don't think he knows how to be different. Like, this is him and he'll always let me down, one shiny, black way or another.

Pause.

Wow, Dad! This is new.

Do I like it?

It's… Um. Well it's very 'you', and um, hah. I think…

No. I don't. To be honest, looks like another one of those toys you buy when you realise how emotionally unfulfilled you are.

Sorry.

I don't want to cry in front of him because it'll really undermine this adult thing I've got going on right now, but I can already feel that lump you usually get growing in your throat, so instead, I just walk away. No words. I just start walking, which is a bit dramatic, I know, but I've already started. This is happening. I can't stop and go back now.

Pause.

Ah! I forgot my—doesn't matter. Keep walking. I'll wait 'til he drives off and then I'll go back for my bags. Yeah. Good.

Pause.

How am I going to get home?

I'll catch a bus.

No, I won't. I don't have any money.

Pause.

Damn…

The Blood on Bloody Blood Ladder
Gretel Vella

Morning. Marion's Bakery. It's all kitsch pastel interiors and jam doughnuts. GRACE, *in a hideous apron and bonnet combo, is shakily transferring vanilla slice from a tray to the display cabinet. The clock ticks. Concentration. Precision. Silence.*

Suddenly she stops, drops her tray on the floor. There's music seeping in from the suburban strip: Fleetwood Mac's 'Rhiannon'. It's creepy. Witchy. Takes her somewhere else.

GRACE: Hello?

> *The door bursts open and* MAISY *sweeps through, in a Stevie Nicks t-shirt and tree leaves from the evening before. In one of her hands is a goon sack, the other, a phone playing music.*

MAISY: ALL YOUR LIFE YOU'VE NEVER SEEN A WOMAN TAKEN BY THE WIND.

GRACE: Maisy.

MAISY: BY THE WIND, GRACE! Come on! Sing it with me, babe!

> MAISY *blows 'wind' in her friend's face.* GRACE *waits, torn, starts to sing:*

GRACE: *Rhi ... aaa—* No. Nah. Let's not do that.

MAISY: Oh, come on! WWSND. What would Stevie Nicks do?

> MAISY *fondles her Stevie t-shirt, kisses it while eyeballing her friend.* GRACE *shuts the music off.*

GRACE: Stevie would open the bakery. That's what she would do.

MAISY: Then take her shoes off, get out her tambourine and play sweet, sweet music to the customers.

GRACE: I don't have a problem with you having an idol, Maisy, but why don't we move away from psychotic seventies queen of rock-and-roll and toward someone who encourages you to make better choices?

MAISY: Like who?

GRACE: I dunno. Michelle Obama.

MAISY: Michelle Obama? She's made *so many* bad choices. Remember that time she kept touching the Queen? Everyone knows you're not meant to touch the Queen.

> *Silence.* GRACE *doesn't know what to do with that.*

GRACE: Just put your uniform on, will you?
MAISY: Wait. I need to tell you something first. I ran all the way here! Without a bra!
GRACE: You've got five minutes, Maisy. Peddo Paul will be here to check in on us soon.

> MAISY *props herself up on the stool near the counter. She reaches an arm into the glass case and extracts a bread roll like her life depends on it.* GRACE *starts to clean up after her.*

MAISY: You might find this hard to believe, but I haven't been home.
GRACE: You've got leaves in your hair.
MAISY: Haven't been home.

> *Pause.*

I've been out by Bloody Blood Ladder.

> GRACE *stops her cleaning. Her eyes glaze over and she's someplace else again.*

Well, it's just Blood Ladder, not Bloody Blood Ladder, but it's really bloody far from this side of town so I renamed it. You remember that creepy ladder they found blood on last year? The one out behind Dalmeny park where there's that tree shaped exactly like a woman sitting on an Ab King Pro?
GRACE: Vaguely remember. I guess.
MAISY: I was there last night with Mike Yang. My bae right now. It's not official or anything. His middle name's 'Alan' and I don't know if that's something I'm into—
GRACE: Just... with haste. The story... please.
MAISY: Well it was unusually cold last night in Dalmeny park. While we were doing hand stuff in the grass. So I tell Mike we should try the old 'kiss and roll' to generate some heat. Well, he wraps his arms around me, we kiss, and roll right into the clearing next to Bloody Blood Ladder. Now, I wanted to get the fuck-ton out of there, because *hello*, blood on a ladder? *That* screams murder.

But before we can even think about rolling back, something really hectic happens. I figure out the bloody blood mystery!

> MAISY *throws her hand in the air, seemingly pointing right at a twitchy* GRACE, *who drops her trays again.* MAISY *kneels up on her stool, starts painting a sort of calligraphy out into the air.*

I beautiful-minded that shit, Grace. Me. A small-town girl, slightly dyslexic, casual employee at Peddo Pete's bakery. Now a local hero.

GRACE: Maisy.

MAISY: Well who should come stumbling through the clearing at that exact moment? None other than—can I put some Stevie music on for this next bit?

GRACE: No.

MAISY: TOD BLOODY RICHARDS with his beautiful golden hair and sex wizard eyes. And he's *all alone…*

> MAISY *starts humming 'Rhiannon'. It's annoying and creepy.*

GRACE: Stop that.

MAISY: So Mike and I have seen Tod in the park earlier in the evening with a cute blonde. But she's not there anymore. Then Mike says to me—get this— 'He comes down here with a different girl every night, and you never see them together again'. So I'm there with all these hectic numbers and images out in front of my beautiful mind: Tod takes girls down to Blood Ladder. You don't see these girls with him again. Mike's rolling me over these uneven hills. Definitely where the bodies are. And then Tod's in the clearing staring up at this blood. And he's… shivering.

GRACE: Shivering?

> *Pause.*

And you're sure this isn't a bit of a stretch? These clues?

MAISY: No. I told you. I beautiful-minded it.

> *Silence.*

GRACE: Well what are you going to do? With this information?

MAISY: Sweet Grace, what have I *done* with this information. I've texted all the girls on the block and we're gonna get down there and throw things at his house.

> MAISY *gets down off her stool.*

So I came here to tell you that story, but also to let you know I won't be in at work today. Thanks for understanding, G-Banger.

She goes for the door. GRACE *opens her mouth a few times, torn.*

GRACE: Wait. Will it be bad?

MAISY: The public naming and shaming? Oh, just awful. He's a womanising murderer. He took Kelly *and* Shelly out last week and mansplained feminism. I'll probably take him to the police station later for a public acknowledgement of my good deed.

GRACE: Right. Ok. Cool… Do you want to… like, maybe… eat a cupcake first?

MAISY: Huh? Like one of the ones that's fallen on the floor?

GRACE: Just any one.

MAISY: Why? You never let me do that.

MAISY *goes to the cabinet. She picks up a cupcake, raises it to her mouth, watches* GRACE *twitch.*

It seems to me a little like you're trying to delay something here. With this cupcake thing. My beautiful mind's twitching again.

GRACE: Definitely not. I know! Why don't we dance to some Stevie music like you were doing before? Put on 'Take the Highway'.

MAISY: 'Go your Own Way'.

GRACE: That one.

MAISY: But you always say dancing is for people who carry the insane gene.

GRACE *switches on 'Rhiannon'.* MAISY *isn't sure what to do. She slowly starts to dance, miming a lot of tambourine work.* GRACE *squirms as* MAISY *walks into cabinets, leaps, removes her shoes.*

Come on then, Grace.

GRACE *is listening to the music, in another world again. She takes* MAISY*'s hand, but can't move.*

Hah! I knew it!

GRACE: What?

MAISY: You don't want me to go to the police. You don't want me to be a hero! You want us to preserve this manager / casual workplace power structure—

GRACE: I know where the blood came from and you're wrong! It wasn't Tod.

    MAISY *stops, still for the first time.*

MAISY: But—
GRACE: Well, it *was* Tod. But it was me, too.
MAISY: You? But you're a manager. And probably have OCD. You don't murder people.
GRACE: What? No! No murder!
MAISY: No murder. Ok. Good start.

    GRACE *throws herself onto a stool, stares out the window.*

GRACE: You remember that personal day I took last year? My only personal day ever.
MAISY: Yes. You got bitten by that strange duck that followed you home.
GRACE: I made that up, Maisy. I'd been down at Blood Ladder. With Tod.
MAISY: Tod!?
GRACE: I know. He told me he just wanted to look into my eyes for a few hours!
MAISY: He said that to Kelly and Shelly too.
GRACE: It started out like that. Just eyes. His were this wonderful green and his whites… So white. Like two boiled eggs. There was a full moon that night and I felt like… Well, like that time I tried a long black!
MAISY: Wild.
GRACE: Things got pretty full on pretty quickly. Everything was so warm and there was this like, washing machine in my stomach on the spin cycle, throwing me in all different directions. Before I knew it his hands were moving down. *There*.

    MAISY *is into it. She takes a jam doughnut from the cabinet and takes a huge bite.*

I wanted to tell him to stop, because *down there* was like a random island in the middle of the ocean—uncharted territory that needed hiking gear and a road map to work out. And it was the wrong time, you know? You get me? But I didn't know how to say it. He just kept whispering wildly distracting and poetic things like, 'you're pretty' and 'this is sick'. Then he just did it. Went there. Down there. And before I knew it was over and he was pulling his hand out and stumbling away.

MAISY: And in his haste he tripped, got injured and sprayed blood everywhere. Of course.

GRACE: No. Do you understand what I'm trying to say?

MAISY: No. Not at all. My beautiful mind is tired, Grace.

GRACE: Me. It's coming from me. It's coming from *down there*.

MAISY puts down the jam doughnut.

Oh God. I know. *I know.* I told you! *It was the wrong time.* I couldn't find the right stupid word to make my blood sound sexy and carefree. The heat and his poetry had melted all my common sense away. And suddenly he was telling me I was gross and crazy. That I didn't know what I was doing. And I'm not warm anymore, I'm on fire. Because I'm smart and good things and punctual, so punctual and this guy gets to decide how much I'm worth. So I'm looking at this full moon and a song clicks on in my head. It's creepy and familiar and kind of hypnotic. And before my brain can make sense of what I'm doing, I'm clinging to the rungs of blood ladder and heaving myself to the top.

She starts to sing a little in between her words.

Rhiannon. Rhiaaanon. And I'm asking myself what fucking Stevie Nicks would do as I reach the summit, see Tod in the distance. Then I take my hand, put it down my pants and smear the blood across everything. *Rhiaa-nnon.* And a fifth of my brain is screaming 'Yes! Go girl!' while the other louder four-fifths are bellowing 'I've smeared my fucking period over a piece of concrete like a psycho maniac. I'm that girl'.

Pause.

Then after, people in town start talking about the blood, creating these stupid myths like it's been there for centuries. Like our forefathers bled on ladders two hundred years ago. And as they talk I know that if Tod squeals, the lining of my uterus will go down in the history of a place that never forgets.

Silence. Terrible silence. MAISY *takes a while.*

This is your fault! If you hadn't planted that psycho Stevie shit in my head—
MAISY: This is hectic. That blood smear is like… Like when dudes pee on walls or spit on walls, or excrete a fluid on a wall—to show they own things. You out-Stevied even Stevie. You pulled a hella gangsta, tribal 'fuck you' move and took back that silo with your lady juice. Like a cat in the night, like a bird in flight, like a witch on a broomstick.

> GRACE *gives* MAISY *a look that stops that train of thought.*
> MAISY *puts an arm round her friend.*

Seems to me like you're afraid of what you did, Grace. That it was psycho, or something. The way I see it, there's a Stevie in all of us, you know? Waiting to get out. That's why I like her. But she's not the bit where we're psycho at all. She's the bit where we can be who we wanna be when we damn well want to be it. She's the bit where we're brave. Kind of. Something shit like that.
GRACE: Ok. Yeah. You just made a lot of sense.
MAISY: You sound surprised. *Mazel tov*, my friend. Apprentice becomes master.
GRACE: I'm sorry. That you don't have a case anymore.
MAISY: Nonsense!

> MAISY *starts to collect her things, takes a swig of her wine.*

GRACE: Where are you going?
MAISY: To Tod's? He's still an arsehole, isn't he?

> MAISY *picks up a bag of rock cakes.*

GRACE: But what if he tells?
MAISY: That's what the rock cakes are for.
GRACE: A bribe?
MAISY: Oh, my sweet Grace.

> MAISY *pegs a rock cake at the wall. The thing's exactly as the name would suggest. Like a rock.*

GRACE: Jesus.

> GRACE *lets* MAISY *leave. We hear 'Rhiannon' play again as the door shuts. The source of the music is unknown. Like it's magic. Like Stevie the psycho queen herself has summoned it to do so.*

Author Biographies

Alexander Lee-Rekers

Alexander is a writer, director and composer. Setting aside a career path as a classical violinist, he left the orchestra pit to study at AFTRS, where he completed the inaugural year of the Foundation Diploma before transitioning into theatre via a two-year tenure as AV Director of the University of Sydney Arts Revue. Alexander completed his MFA in Writing for Performance at NIDA. Towards the end of his studies, he began to consult on shows as a dramaturg; since graduating he has worked in this capacity for productions at Bondi Feast, Sydney Fringe, the Old 505 and the Old Fitz Theatre. Alexander continues his work as a playwright and splits his time between theatre, television (for which he writes the Disney Channel program 'Hanging With') and teaching (for both NIDA and ATYP).

Pippa Ellams

Pippa is a writer and performer from Western Sydney. Her first play *The Carousel* was shortlisted for the Rodney Seaborn Playwrights Award in 2015. During 2017 the play was produced at Shopfront Arts Co-op while Pippa was a Resident Artist there, followed by a remount at Belvoir St Theatre (downstairs) in June 2017. *The Carousel* is set to tour in 2018, beginning with Merrigong Theatre Company. Pippa participated in the Propel Initiative, created by Q Theatre and ATYP to support young Western Sydney writers. She is also a participant in National Theatre of Parramatta's Playwrights of Parramatta group.

David Stewart

David is a Brisbane-based writer and performer, and co-creator of the electro-musical comedy trio The Architects of Sound (Brisbane Festival, Fringe World, Melbourne International Comedy Festival, Melbourne Fringe). Recent playwriting credits include *Numb* (Playlab), *Non-Vegan Hoagies and Other Signs of the Impending Apocalypse* (ATYP

National Studio), *An Intimate Evening with the Architects of Sound* (Wonderland, Melbourne Fringe Festival, Woodford Folk Festival), *Slug* (Rock Surfers Theatre Company) and *The Art of Conversation* (Short + Sweet, winner: best comedy). David graduated from the NIDA Writing for Performance MFA in 2015.

Gretel Vella

Gretel is a Sydney-based writer and director, and a current graduate of NIDA's MFA in Writing for Performance. She was selected for ATYP's National Studio and Fresh Ink Mentoring programs during 2017, and has recently been awarded an ATYP co-commission for her play *Bathory Begins*. Gretel's screenplays, 'Carking It' (TV) and *Elsie Shrew* (feature) were longlisted for the Australian Writers' Guild Primetime and Insite writing competitions in 2017. She currently writes for Channel Nine's medical drama, 'Doctor Doctor', and is co-artistic director of The Louise Frequency with Emme Hoy. She is also an associate artist with Glitterbomb, Sydney.

Joseph Brown

Joseph is a theatremaker who grew up in Armidale, NSW. After completing his Bachelor degree in performing arts at Monash University in 2012, Joseph moved on to a MFA in Writing for Performance at NIDA. While there, he wrote two screenplays: *The End of Hawke Street* and *86'd*. Joseph's other writing and directing credits include *A Midsummer Night's Dream* (Monash Shakespeare Company), *You Walk Away* (Melbourne Fringe), *Tuck in the Corners* (MUST, La Mama) and *Tensions: Curated Works* (MUST).

Liz Hobart

Liz is a Sydney-based writer for both stage and screen. After completing her Bachelor of Arts (Writing) at Macquarie University, she went on to undertake an MFA in Writing for Performance at NIDA. While there, Liz wrote the feature film screenplay (*The Trove*), a TV pilot ('Mercy'), three short films (*The Picnic*, *Muddied Matter* and *Spent Alone*) and a musical adaptation of *Dot and the Kangaroo*. In 2017 Liz participated in the National Studio at ATYP. Her play *Snap Season* was also staged as part of the Sydney Fringe Festival. In 2018, Liz's productions include *Intersection: Chrysalis* (ATYP) and *Lie With Me* at (Old 505 Theatre).

Madelaine Nunn

Madelaine graduated with a Bachelor of Fine Arts (Theatre Practice) from the VCA in 2015. Since graduating she has been nominated for two Green Room Awards for Best Ensemble, and has co-founded the female-led theatre company *Three Birds Theatre*. Madelaine has written for and performed in Poppy Seed Theatre Festival, CRACK Theatre Festival, Metanoia and the Adelaide and the Melbourne Fringe, and has toured with Regional Arts Victoria. In 2016, Madelaine was part of ATYP's Fresh Ink mentorship program.

Madison Behringer

Madison is a Sydney-based writer, director, actor and theatremaker. While completing her Performance degree at the University of Wollongong, Madison directed several short plays for local independent theatre companies, including devising and producing a political theatre piece investigating the media coverage of the 2014 Sydney Siege (OUW's SIP Program). In 2014 she wrote and directed the full-length play *Happily Ever After* at the Lighthouse Theatre. Madison seeks to explore real-life experiences in the theatre, and enjoys writing realistic characters into her work. Outside of writing, her interests include two-minute noodles, her dog, and looking on realestate.com at houses she can't afford.

Phoebe Sullivan

Phoebe Sullivan is a Perth-based artist, writer, and theatremaker. Graduating in 2016 from the Performance Making course at WAAPA, Phoebe seeks to make new work that is an exploration of language and the body, the innate desire to belong, and the private, often unappealing, sides to ourselves that prevent this from happening. Her practice extends locally and nationally, working and undertaking residencies with companies such as ATYP, Queensland Theatre, Metro Arts, Black Swan State Theatre Company, PICA, pvi collective,

Playwriting Australia and Blue Room Theatre. Phoebe aims to making new Australian work that explores themes and issues relevant to contemporary culture; recovering lost sensations, our bodies, empathy, and placing it at the heart of it all.

Julia Rorke

Julia's theatre credits include her acclaimed solo theatre comedy show, *Don't Be a Cunt This is How*, which she wrote, directed and performed (Adelaide Fringe, Melbourne International Comedy Festival, Edinburgh Fringe) and her newest show *Not Another Fucked Bitch In India* (Sydney Fringe Comedy, Tandanya Arts, The Malthouse). She is currently in development with the ABC to adapt these for screen. Julia's film credits include her web series 'Loose Bitch', 'Tony Fitzgerald's Cult Following' (Felicity Pickering, Flickrfest) and 'Anti-Adult' (Jason Kos). In 2014 she directed Adam Cass's *Bock Kills Her Father* at 107 Projects. Other theatre acting credits include *Tell It Like It Isn't*, *The One Sure Thing*, *Animal Farm* and *Bite Me* (AYTP), *Vernon God Little* (New Theatre), *80 Minutes No Interval* (Red Line Productions/Old Fitz), Festival of New Writing (Griffin Theatre) Harvest Festival (Harvest Presents/ATYP).

Harry Goodlet

Harry Goodlet is an emerging writer, director and performer from Perth. He has been involved in numerous amateur productions within the Perth independent scene with a strong emphasis on writing and directing comedy. He completed Blue Room Theatre's Sustained Playwriting program in 2017 before moving into the field of screenwriting. As of 2018, he will reside in Melbourne, studying at the Victorian College of the Arts.

Mentor Biographies

Michele Lee

Michele is an Asian-Australian playwright and theatremaker working across stage and audio. Her works are about female identity, otherness, intimacy and chaotic worlds, usually through a non-white perspective. She has been commissioned by Radio National, Next Wave Festival, Darwin Festival, Platform Youth Theatre, St Martins Youth Arts Centre, Westside Circus, Platform Youth Theatre, Arts House, Griffin Theatre, Sydney Theatre Company, Melbourne Theatre Company and Malthouse Theatre. She is currently working on new plays about single women and female security guards. Michele has been script advisor or mentor to the Home project; the Ribcage Collective; and to student writers through her residency this year at Union House Theatre. She has been a resident at the Playwrights' Center (USA); a WrICE fellow (China/Melbourne); Co.Lab (Malthouse Theatre); Ian Reed; and an Asialink resident in Laos. She has assessed scripts for Playwriting Australia and for the AWGIE Awards. Michele has also been invited to numerous conferences and events to discuss diversity in theatre. She is the 2015 recipient of the Malcolm Robertson Prize for her new play *Going Down*. She is the winner of the 2016-17 Queensland Premiers' Drama Award for her play *Rice*, which was presented by Queensland Theatre Company, Griffin Theatre and Hothouse Theatre in 2017. Her radio play *See how the leaf people run* won an AWGIE Award in 2013. Michele's audio theatre work *Talon Salon* was presented in Next Wave Festival and re-mounted by invitation for You Are Here Festival and Darwin Festival. Michele's memoir *Banana Girl* was published by Transit Lounge in 2013.

Stephen Carleton

Stephen is an award-winning Brisbane-based writer who has had his work produced by Queensland Theatre Company, La Boite, Sydney Theatre Company, Griffin, JUTE, Darwin Theatre Company, Brisbane Powerhouse and La Mama. He is the winner of the 2016 Matilda Award for Best New Australian Work for *Bastard Territory*, the 2015 Griffin Award for *The Turquoise Elephant*, and the 2004/5 Patrick White Playwrights' Award for *Constance Drinkwater and the Final Days of Somerset*, which also won the New York New Dramatists' Award, and was shortlisted for an AWGIE Award and the Queensland Literary Award. *Bastard Territory* was also shortlisted for the Queensland Literary Award and the Patrick White Playwrights' Award, under the title *1975*. His play *The Narcissist* was also shortlisted for the Queensland Literary Award in 2008. His musical comedy *Joh for PM* (co-written with Paul Hodge) opened the Queensland Music Festival at the Brisbane Powerhouse in July 2017. Stephen is co-Artistic Director of Knock-em-Down Theatre, and has written and produced plays that have been toured there in conjunction with JUTE since 2004. He is a Senior Lecturer in Drama at the University of Queensland, where he teaches courses in playwriting, dramaturgy, Australian drama and theatre history, specialising in postcolonial and Gothic theatre. Stephen was also the 2016 co-Chair of the National Playwrights' Committee.

Mary Rachel Brown

Mary is the recipient of the Lysicrates Prize, the Rodney Seaborn Award, the Max Afford Award and the Griffin Award. Her works for the stage include *Inside Out* (Christine Dunstan Productions), *Die Fledermaus* (Sydney Conservatorium of Music), *National Security and the Art of Taxidermy* (Glynn Nicholas Group), *All My Sleep and Waking* (TRS), *The Dapto Chaser* (Apocalypse / Merrigong Theatre Company / Griffin Independent), *Silent Night* (Darlinghurst Theatre Company) and *Last Letters* (Australian War Memorial). Mary is currently under commission with Griffin Theatre Company and the University of Wollongong. Mary's TV credits include sketch writing for 'The Elegant Gentleman's Guide to Knife Fighting' for the ABC and several episodes of 'Home and Away' for Channel 7. Mary's play *Permission to Spin* hits the stage at the Old Fitz in 2018.

Join the ATYP family.

All of ATYP's productions and programs are supported by our in-house learning experts, who design and deliver programs that connect our programs to schools and teachers nationally and internationally.

Working closely with artists and creative professionals, our learning department gives schools and students clear insight into all stages of the theatre-making process: from script development and production design to performance and post-show analysis.

ATYP takes learning and education beyond the theatre and classroom and delivers it to every corner of Australia. In 2018 our touring monologues production, *Monologues Now!* will hit the road, travelling to schools around the country, bringing a unique performance and workshop experience to students in regional and remote communities. And if we can't see you in person, you can still join the action online by tuning in to our free live streamed performances, suitable for various stages for students and teachers across Australia.

The ATYP theatre experience is different from any other in the world. Students can see their peers on stage, then audition to be in a show themselves. They can come for a workshop with an ATYP artist, then join in the development of a new work. In fact, without even leaving your classroom you can see a professional-quality performance then unpack its themes and ideas with our excellent online resources.

Don't miss these exceptional opportunities. Make sure ATYP is at the top of your list for drama education in 2018.

Do you teach young people? Contact ATYP Learning today!

Phone: 02 9270 2400
Email: education@atyp.com.au
Website: http://www.atyp.com.au/education

More ATYP titles from Currency Press

Voices Project 2012: Tell It Like It Isn't / The One Sure Thing
A short, sharp, evocative collection of monologues written by some of Australia's leading young and established playwrights. *(Ebook only)*

The Voices Project 2013: Out of Place
A collection of seven-minute monologues with young characters that laugh, tease and tell stories to make your toes curl. What happens when people are placed just outside their comfort zone.
978-0-86819-978-8

The Voices Project 2014: Bite Me
This collection of thirteen monologues serves a mouth-watering banquet of work exploring our relationship with food. Funny, warm, irreverent and cheeky, this is a feast for the senses.
978-1-92500-507-3, or as an ebook

The Voices Project 2015: Between Us
The latest instalment of The Voices Project—the overwhelmingly successful annual program of monologues developed by ATYP, written by young people, performed by young actors around the country.
978-1-92500-535-6, or as an ebook

The Voices Project 2016: All Good Things
Directed by one of Australia's masters of new writing, Iain Sinclair, this final season explores departures. *The Voices Project* has given a generation monologues that speak their language.
978-1-92500-579-0, or as an ebook

The Voices Project: Encore Edition
This selection takes the reader through the themes that have been explored in the Voices Project over the years, telling the stories of Australia. By turns witty, touching and chilling, the monologues explore, deconstruct and subvert perceptions of modern Australian life.
978-1-92500-557-8, or as an ebook

Intersection
Intricately drawn by Australia's leading young writers, this collection of short stories plays out across the same town, creating a glorious map of the connections we form and the experiences we have when we're seventeen.
978-1-76062-084-4, or as an ebook

www.currency.com.au

Visit Currency Press' website now to:

- Order books
- Browse through our full list of titles including plays, screenplays, theory and reference/criticism, performance handbooks, educational texts and more
- Choose a play for your school or performance group by cast specs
- Seek performance rights
- Find out about performing arts news and sign up for our newsletter
- For students: read our study guides
- For teachers: access free curriculum information and teacher notes

We are also on Facebook and Instagram (@currencypress). Join the conversation!

The performing arts publisher

www.ingramcontent.com/pod-product-compliance
Lightning Source LLC
Chambersburg PA
CBHW050034090426
42735CB00022B/3477